The Trial of Charles I

The Trial of Charles I

A Documentary History

Edited by
David Lagomarsino and
Charles T. Wood

Published for Dartmouth College by
University Press of New England
Hanover and London

Printed in the United States of America
∞
Library of Congress Cataloging-in-Publication Data
The trial of Charles I: a documentary history/edited by David
    Lagomarsino, Charles T. Wood.
            p.   cm.
    Includes bibliographical references.
    ISBN 0–87451–500–9. — ISBN 0–87451–499–1 (pbk.)
    1. Charles I, King of England, 1600–1649—Trials, litigation, etc.
2. Trials (Treason)—England—London. 3. Great Britain—Politics
and government—1642–1649.   I. Lagomarsino, David.   II. Wood,
Charles T.   III. Dartmouth College.
KD372.C53T75   1989
345.42'0231—dc20   89–40356
[344.205231]   CIP

5 4 3

Contents

Illustrations

The Trial
of Charles I

Introduction

On 1 January 1649, what remained of the House of Commons after Pride's Purge passed an ordinance for the trial of Charles I and transmitted it to the Lords for their approval. The proposed ordinance named one hundred fifty commissioners to manage the proceedings, at least twenty of whom were to serve as a High Court of Justice to determine whether Charles had subverted "the ancient laws and liberties of this nation"—whether, in brief, he had committed treason. The court was to have no more than a month in which to render its verdict, but to assist it in its labors the House also passed a resolution stating "that the Lords and Commons in Parliament assembled do declare and adjudge that by the fundamental laws of this kingdom it is treason in the King of England for the time being to levy war against the Parliament and the Kingdom of England."

When the Lords refused their concurrence on 2 January, the Commons decided to proceed without them, eliminating lords from the list of commissioners and reducing their number to one hundred thirty-five. The basis for this action came in a resolution passed on the fourth in which it was affirmed

that the Commons of England in Parliament assembled do declare that the people are, under God, the original of all just power; and do also declare that the Commons of England in Parliament assembled, being chosen by and representing the people, have the supreme power in this nation; and do also declare that whatsoever is enacted or declared for law by the Commons in Parliament assembled hath the force of law, and all the people of this nation are included thereby, although the consent and concurrence of King or House of Peers be not had thereunto.

Given this resolution, the new definition of treason, and the nature of the civil war just past, the outcome of the trial seems a foregone conclusion. On 27 January, and after "serious and mature deliberation," the members of the High Court found themselves "fully satisfied in their judgments and consciences": Charles I had indeed been "guilty of levying war against the said Parliament and people," as a result of which he was to "be put to death by the severing of his head from his body." Two days later, fifty-nine commissioners signed a warrant declaring that insofar as "Charles Stuart, King of England, is and standeth convicted, attainted, and condemned of High Treason and other high crimes," the sentence was to be carried out "in the open street before Whitehall, upon the morrow, being the thirtieth day of this instant month of January, between the hours of ten in the morning and five in the afternoon of the same day, with full effect." And when, on that morrow, the warrant took its full effect, opponents of monarchy were doubtless confident that, in the words of the new Great Seal of England that the Commons had approved on 9 January, this event marked the beginning of "the First Year of Freedom by God's Blessing Restored."

Even granted the fact that revolutions are never very pretty affairs, there is little about this one which suggests that God's blessing had had much to do with it. Baldly stated, the plain fact was that Charles I had lost a civil war and was therefore made to pay the price for his loss. The war had started in midsummer of 1642 with disorganized skirmishes at such places as Beverley, but it took on a formal character in late August of that year when Charles raised the royal standard at Nottingham. With that action he gave legal being to the army needed to oppose the parliamentary forces then forming against him, but the succeeding years brought little success either to Charles or to royalist generals such as Prince Rupert. Especially after the creation of the New Model Army (1645), early royal victories such as Edgehill (1642) gave way to crushing defeats such as Naseby (1645), and by May 1646, when Charles surrendered to the Scots, it looked as though the war was effectively over.

Nevertheless, achieving peace proved exceedingly difficult. The King believed in the rightness of his cause to the depths of his being, and when, in December 1647, he reached an agreement with Scottish commissioners, he had grounds for believing that with Scottish assistance his still-numerous English supporters might yet prevail. Moreover, his enemies were in obvious disarray. What may be termed the revolutionary party found itself increasingly split into warring factions, moderates versus radicals. By late 1647, it also appeared that the New Model Army had become little more than a contentious debating society, one in which generals spent most of their time searching for ways to introduce a modicum of reality into some of the wilder dreams of the enlisted ranks.

By spring of 1648, the result was renewed civil war of heightened ferocity. As one of the more militant groups explained after vowing its support to Oliver Cromwell, "it was our duty, if ever the Lord brought us back to peace, to call Charles Stuart, that man of blood, to an account for the blood he had shed, and the mischief he had done to his utmost, against the Lord's cause and people." By autumn, moreover, the opportunity for testing these views had arisen. With the Scots defeated and the rest of his forces unfit for combat, on 18 September Charles began negotiations on the Isle of Wight with representatives of Parliament, a body that then contained a Presbyterian majority of moderate outlook.

Negotiations again proved difficult—Charles was, for example, reluctant to give up bishops and refused to take the Calvinist Covenant—but when, on 2 October, the representatives rejected his every proposal, the King backed down at least partially. He now agreed that there should be limitations on episcopal jurisdiction and that Parliament should have control of the military for twenty years, not to mention permanent control over affairs in Ireland. Nevertheless, because Parliament itself rejected these terms on 27

October, even though its commissioners did not leave until a month later, it remained unclear whether what both sides called the Treaty of Newport could be given an acceptable form.

At this point, however, other factors came into play. In particular, while negotiations were still proceeding, the Army—and especially that portion of it led by Henry Ireton—showed increasing restlessness. For people of Ireton's outlook, any attempt to negotiate with Charles was an abomination, so in October he drew up the "Remonstrance of the Army." Appealing to the "sovereignty of the People," he demanded a speedy trial for the King, a man whom he saw as being in no way above the law. Future Kings were to be recognized only "upon the election of, and as upon trust from, the people," and they were further to renounce their right to veto parliamentary actions.

On 7 November, the Army's Council of Officers considered the Remonstrance under the presidency of Thomas, Lord Fairfax, a man of more moderate outlook than Ireton, one still interested in and committed to a settlement with the King. The result was a compromise, one in which a treaty with Charles was still to be pursued, but with the full participation of the Army. Its representatives were to insist on certain provisions dear to Ireton such as biennial Parliaments, a redistribution of its seats, and a new Council of State more independent of the royal will. But Charles proved no more receptive to these proposals than he had to the earlier ones of Parliament, rejecting them totally on 17 November. The next day, the Army made public its revised Remonstrance, thereby transforming the situation into one of outright confrontation. The die was now cast.

Two weeks later, on 1 December, soldiers removed the King from Newport to Hurst Castle; within twenty-four hours troops began to enter London. When, on 4–5 December, Parliament denounced Charles's seizure and voted that his answers to its proposals at Newport should be considered as a possible basis for settlement, the Army's response was immediate: On the morning of the sixth, troops under the command of Colonel Thomas Pride prevented roughly one hundred forty members of the House of Commons from entering their place of meeting, and more were barred later. Some members were quickly imprisoned or "secured". Others, a greater number, were merely "secluded"—that is, allowed a restricted liberty while still being denied entrance and involvement in the Commons' affairs, but the fact remains that this purge effectively removed from the scene that majority of moderates that continued to favor a negotiated settlement.

Although the troops in London were still nominally under the command of Fairfax, he participated in none of these actions. That he opposed them is nowhere more graphically demonstrated than in his refusal to serve on the High Court of Justice, a refusal dramatically underscored on 20 January when, in an outburst at Westminster Hall, a masked Lady Fairfax protested even the mention of her husband's name in any way that would associate him with the trial. On the other hand, Oliver Cromwell took a different position. He, too, had not been consulted before Pride's Purge, but when he arrived in London some ten hours later, he expressed approval of all that had occurred.

In the course of December, this cautious approval was to harden into a grimmer resolve, one in which Charles again played his usual stubborn role. Just before Christmas, the King was taken from Hurst Castle to Windsor. At that point, Cromwell apparently hoped that a trial could still be postponed, so, with that in mind, he agreed to one last attempt to reach a compromise with the King. This one called for a purely ceremonial monarchy, one in which Charles and his successors would enjoy no more than symbolic powers. When, however, Charles refused even to discuss the matter, Cromwell finally decided that the only solution lay in trial and death, a death that would end the monarchy in its entirety. As he reputedly put it on 19 January when defending the judicial proceedings: "I tell you we will cut off his head with the crown on it." As, indeed, they did.

Charles I was not the first English King to lose his life and his throne, but he is unique in having participated in a public trial for which significant source materials survive. This book is an amalgam of those sources, and their testimony makes it possible to understand not only what happened but also, and more importantly, just why it happened. In a sense, of course, exploration of this latter issue seems almost irrelevant. After all, Charles had lost an increasingly bitter civil war; he had showed himself totally incapable of coming to any sort of accommodation with his enemies; and those enemies, more and more militant, finally decided that their one hope of ending the dispute lay in severing their sovereign's head from his body. Although they attempted to act under cover of legality, their appeals to such notions as the sovereignty of the people will strike doubters

as pure rationalizations of the moment, attempts to justify the unjusti-
fiable. Their actions can be seen, then, as little more than brute force,
brutally applied.

To illustrate the point, one has only to consider the law of treasons under which Charles I was found guilty, a law which, incidental-
ly, had never allowed the accused to have counsel. From the time of
its first statutory definition in 1352, this law held that the person
guilty of treason was one who "compasses or imagines the death of
our Lord the King," one who "makes war against our said Lord the
King in his Kingdom, or is an adherent of enemies to our Lord the
King in the Kingdom." How, then, was Charles himself to be found
guilty of treason against the King? He had not committed suicide, nor
had he carried on war against himself. Rather, the explanation lies
solely in the ex post facto redefinition of 1 January 1649, the one in
which it was declared that "it is treason in the King of England . . .
to levy war against the Parliament and Kingdom of England."

Furthermore, if such evidence is not enough, Charles I himself
supplied a great deal more in a speech that John Bradshaw, Lord
President of the High Court of Justice, forbade him to give on 22
January—but which was, significantly, published shortly thereafter in
spite of Bradshaw's objections. For Charles, the issues were very
clear. The Bible enjoined all subjects to obey their King, and insofar as
it was also the King who gave expression to the law in his judgments,
it was only with a King that subjects could enjoy true liberty as expe-
rienced under the law. How, then, could the House of Commons create a High Court of Justice against the King when the Commons
themselves were not a court? And on what basis could the Commons
claim genuinely to represent the people of England? The House of
Lords was excluded from the trial; indeed, even "the major part" of
the Commons had been prevented from participating as a result of
Pride's Purge. It followed, therefore, not only that Charles refused the
High Court's jurisdiction, but also that he had to claim that anything
it chose to do would be in derogation of the basic liberties of the people of England.

Anyone who has ever seen these events dramatized surely knows
why actors so covet the part of Charles, for it has an inherent majesty
seemingly based on the experience of the ages. On the other hand,
what such dramatizations miss is the extent to which those opposed
to Charles drew on sources much more substantial—and of much

greater antiquity—than their own selfish passions. On stage, for example, the Lord President of the High Court John Bradshaw often comes across as a man of less than judicial temperament, but in fact his judgments frequently drew on views that had a distinguished past, though a tumultuous future.

Bradshaw's chance for glory came on 27 January 1649 when, before the actual sentencing of the King, he seized the opportunity to explain just why it was that subjects had the right, nay the duty, to resist those whom others might regard as their sovereigns. Bradshaw's citations were frequent—Scripture backed up by Cicero, Magna Carta, and three distinguished English jurists, Henry de Bracton, Sir John Fortescue, and Sir Edward Coke—and he used them to argue that the law was any King's superior. Further, although it was true that Parliament was "the sovereign and highest court of justice, . . . the sole maker of the law," the real "parent or author of the law" remained "the people of England." Thus, if the law was superior to the King, that meant, in effect, that his was no more than an office to be held in trust, an argument Bradshaw found to be in accord with the "law of old," not Charles's "law of yesterday." Little wonder, then, that "Parliaments were ordained . . . to redress the grievances of the people" since, as "the sole maker of the law," they alone could rightly claim superiority to everything and everybody other than that ultimate sovereign, "the people of England."

Over the centuries, few analysts have taken Bradshaw's arguments seriously, but a review of the historical record suggests that his views, although expressed in the heat of the moment, had far more behind them than pure expediency. In an immediate sense, many of them sprang from Leveller ideas most fully set forth in that "Agreement of the People" which had first taken shape in the Army's Putney Debates of 1647. Filled with notions of a social contract and popular sovereignty, this document resurfaced at the trial, though in the more cautious form devised by a General Council of the Army far less anxious to bring in the reign of God's saints than to insure that the sensible rule of His propertied class would long continue.

Nevertheless, of much greater importance to Bradshaw's argument—and, indeed, to the whole case against Charles—was another stream of thought, the antiquity and respectability of which helps explain just why the High Court of Justice truly believed it had the legitimate authority to try its King. As far back as 1327, in pronouncing the deposition of Edward II, the Archbishop of Canterbury Walter Reynolds had taken as his justifying text the old Carolingian adage *Vox populi, vox Dei,* "The voice of the people is the voice of God." In so doing, he was not merely rationalizing. On the contrary, he had in mind Matthew 18:20, the passage in which Christ assures His Apostles that "where two or three are gathered together in my name, there am I in the midst of them." As interpreted by generations of canon lawyers, this verse had come to mean that an assembly of normally fallible men could speak with the voice of the Holy Spirit, and that any decision made by their "better and wiser part" would therefore prove inerrant, even though that part did not command a majority. Possibly more to the point, those lawyers had further held that any such body, so assembled and so constituted, had the power to judge the crimes even of popes or kings who normally ruled over it.

Revolutionary in practical politics in 1327, this idea had been reaffirmed in the deposition of Richard II in 1399 and subsequently became almost a commonplace in all the depositional activities of the fifteenth century. In the English version of this theory, any fully representative assembly of the clergy and people—in other words, what most people would have thought of as Parliament—derived its powers not from the King, but from God and the realm; as a result, it could exercise the highest possible earthly authority. It was hardly by chance, then, that Henry VIII used the authority of Parliament to break with Rome since, as one of his monastic receivers put it, "[A]n act of Parliament made in the realm for the common wealth of the same ought rather to be observed within the same realm than any general council [of the Church]. And I think that the Holy Ghost is as verily present at such an act as it ever was at any general council."

Moreover, given the prevalence of these ideas, it seems understandable that some men should have begun to conceive even of treason in potentially new terms. In 1404, for example, the Commons asked Henry IV to find guilty of treason anyone who "kills or murders a man who has . . . come to Parliament under your protection." Although many doubtless considered this request to be little more than an extension of the security that the statute of treasons afforded to Henry's own person, others recognized that acceptance of this petition would effectively redefine treason as a crime against the Kingdom, not the King. Small wonder, then, that Henry's response

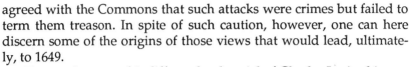

agreed with the Commons that such attacks were crimes but failed to term them treason. In spite of such caution, however, one can here discern some of the origins of those views that would lead, ultimately, to 1649.

To put the case a bit differently, the trial of Charles I raised issues that were far from new, and they were not without a future. Furthermore, those who were forced to deal with them were, as the record makes clear, pressed to do so under revolutionary circumstances that gave precious little opportunity for clear and sagacious thought. They wanted instantly to implement that purification of public morals that was so much a part of their revolution, but how were they to do it? Would the Army take over? Would the Scots or Prince Rupert invade? How were the Commons to respond to the Lords' refusal to participate, and would they be able to develop the legal and parliamentary procedures needed to deal with questions of such unprecedented political volatility? Where would they find the money needed to pay for it all, not least the wages owed to the restless Army? And how, in the end, were those whom the next generation would term regicides to justify their actions, not just to the protesting Dutch and anxious Scots, but to themselves and posterity?

The wonder, really, is that in the midst of this total confusion both sides found the capacity to keep their wits about them, often with stunning clarity. When Bradshaw argued that the people alone had created kingship as an office to be held in trust, he found his position countered by Charles's objection that it was, rather, "a trust committed to me by God." Conversely, when Charles sought to enlarge on the point, insisting that his title had come to him purely "by old and lawful descent," Bradshaw remained unmoved. Since Charles accepted the view of such medieval jurists as Glanvill and Bracton that "only God can make an heir," he was confident that the fact that England had been "an hereditary kingdom for near these thousand years" proved the uniquely divine origins of his own authority. Unimpressed, Bradshaw could then respond, and with total historical accuracy, that if the prisoner at the bar was "the twenty-fourth King from William, called the Conqueror[,] you shall find more than one half of them . . . come merely from the state and not merely upon the point of descent." Thus were the claims of divine heredity deftly undercut.

On the other hand, this exchange did not in the end favor

Bradshaw. In the previous year, the Lord President had been made a
Serjeant at Law, and, as a state lawyer, he seems to have assumed his
monarch's knowledge of the law. As a result, when he went on to cite
an opinion from "Of the Title of the House of York," a work by Henry
VI's Chief Justice Sir John Fortescue, he did not so identify it. Rather,
he simply said: "And truly, sir, . . . a grave and learned judge in his
time, and well known to you, once said . . . that although there was
such a thing as descent many times, yet the Kings of England ever
held the greatest assurance of their titles when they were declared by
Parliament."

Denied an opportunity for immediate response, three days later
Charles found it possible to say what he thought, in his speech from
the scaffold. Although Bradshaw had not mentioned it, Fortescue's
argument had included a quotation from St. Augustine's *City of God*, a
quotation in which this greatest of all the Fathers of the Church had
asked with Cicero, "What are kingdoms without justice but a great
robbery?" Because Charles had already received the last rites of his
Church, he found himself "in charity," morally forbidden to speak ill
either of Bradshaw or anyone else. Nevertheless, in his last moments
he still found it possible to demonstrate his knowledge not just of
Fortescue, but also of the full Augustinian passage from which that
exiled Chief Justice of a deposed King had so briefly quoted:

Now, sirs, . . . you are out of the way, for certainly all the
way you ever have had . . . is in the way of conquest.
Certainly this is an ill way. For conquest, sirs, in my opinion
is never just [since], . . . if it be only matter of conquest, then
it is a great robbery; as a pirate said to Alexander the Great
that he was the great robber, he [the pirate] was but a petty
robber. And so, sirs, I do think the way that you are in is
much out of the way.

Charles, then, fought on to the last, and not unsuccessfully. For
him, after all, the stakes were obvious, though not just in personal
terms. On the contrary, since his own fate was already determined,
the game had become one of ensuring that through his own martyr-
dom the monarchy itself would endure. And in this game he was ultimately to prove victorious, for both in his ungiven speech of 22
January and in the nobility with which he endured the savagery of his

end, he displayed the kind of transcendent simplicity of purpose that practically guaranteed that, one day, his son Charles II would regain and restore the throne.

As for his opponents, men such as John Bradshaw and the more redoubtable Oliver Cromwell, history has proved less kind. And understandably so, since they were men who killed their King. On the other hand, long after doubters have stopped stressing the power politics that led to Charles's fate, the more reflective among us will continue to ponder the sovereignty of the people and all those other seventeenth-century ideas that have so shaped the modern world. To say this is surely not to grace Cromwell and his supporters with that martyr's crown won and worn by their royal opponent, but it is, perhaps, to assert that ideas have a life of their own, quite independent of those who, for whatever reason, first gave them expression. Both John Bradshaw and Oliver Cromwell would doubtless have recoiled in horror if ever they had been forced to confront the modern world, and yet the truth of the matter is that their own thoughts had not a little to do with the creation of it.

About the Documents

This book is not a critical edition of the records relating to the trial and execution of Charles I; it is, rather, a compilation designed to sketch the narrative of these events and to introduce the important issues they raised. Four types of contemporary documents have been drawn upon: (1) news reports taken from John Rushworth's *Historical Collections* and in turn mostly culled by him from newspapers of the day; (2) extracts from the official records of the House of Commons and High Court of Justice, giving a behind-the-scenes look at what might be called the operational routine of the English Revolution; (3) transcripts of the public sessions of the trial, presenting the exchanges between the King and his judges; and (4) contemporary pamphlets throwing light on particular issues and events. The sources are fully identified at the end of the volume.

In editing the documents, the aim has been to make them accessible to nonspecialists while still preserving their original flavor. Spelling and punctuation have been modernized, a few archaic verbs have been changed, and the occasional textual slip has been silently

repaired. Latin quotations have been translated (perhaps to the detriment of Lord President Bradshaw's aura of erudition), and their sources have been identified wherever possible. Some extraneous references and repetitious materials have been cut where this could be done without distortion. Editorial clarifications are interpolated in brackets, and dates have been adjusted to conform to modern usage. That is, the English at this time computed their years as running from 25 March (Lady Day) through 24 March of what we would consider to be the next calendar year. The effect was that the King's trial and execution were dated as taking place in January, the tenth month of 1648, whereas in this collection the date has been rendered as January 1649.

But no amount of editorial tinkering centuries after the event can disguise the rough urgency these documents still convey. They may be wordy at times, a jarring reminder that committee prose could be as opaque in the age of Milton as it is today; and the dialogue can lapse into the inarticulate, when the players in this courtroom drama were unable to say quite what they meant as elegantly as they wished. Even when their eloquence did break through, we can imagine the inevitable coughing spectators and creaking bleachers in Westminster Hall garbling the nuances while stenographers strained their ears and rushed their pens to take it all down for posterity. But as worried, distracted, and exhausted as the participants in the trial had every excuse to be, their words could sometimes soar with the clarity and poignancy befitting this life-and-death debate over fundamental law and the locus of sovereignty. Even when the documents deal merely with catering arrangements to feed the Lord President, or with searching the cellars under the court for bombs, or with sending someone along to the Tower to fetch "the bright Execution Ax," we sense we are close to great events in the making. Sometimes mundane, sometimes heroic, the following pages chronicle a revolutionary moment in English history.

The Trial of Charles I

Prologue

Negotiations with the King

Friday, 1 December 1648—the House of Commons debates whether to accept the King's most recent concessions as a basis for settling the peace of the kingdom

The House this day heard the report of the commissioners from the Isle of Wight of His Majesty's several concessions, which was read twice over and the greatest part of the day spent in debate thereof. About 2 of the clock in the afternoon they came to the question whether they should now debate whether His Majesty's answers and concessions reported by them are satisfactory or unsatisfactory, and it was resolved in the negative that they would not then debate it further or let the question be put, but that the debate thereof should be resumed tomorrow morning at 9 of the clock.

Saturday, 2 December 1648—the debate continues

This day the House resumed the debate (according to order) of the King's concessions and answers upon the treaty. The debate was very high and took up the whole day, yet they came to no conclusion or any vote passed, but put off the further debate till Monday morning.

Monday, 4 December 1648—a report reaches the Commons that the Army has abducted the King

This day the House of Commons (according to former order) took into further debate His Majesty's concessions, whether satisfactory or not, about which they spent all Friday and Saturday last week, and not one vote passed and the question in no way likely to be decided this day.

Being upon this debate, a letter came to the Speaker from the officers deputed by Colonel Hammond to take the charge of His Majesty in the Isle of Wight, that His Majesty was removed thence to Hurst Castle by order of the General [i.e., Lord Fairfax] and Council of the Army.

The House upon reading this letter entered into a new debate and voted that the seizing upon the person of the King and carrying him prisoner to Hurst Castle was without the advice or consent of the House. After this, again they debated of His Majesty's concessions and sat all the day and night but came to no resolution till the next morning.

Tuesday, 5 December 1648—the Commons accept the King's concessions while the Army extends its occupation of London

This morning early (the House having sat all night) the question was put and voted that His Majesty's concessions to the propositions of Parliament upon the treaty are sufficient grounds for settling the peace of the kingdom.

Some more forces of the Army came to London this day and yesterday. They still quarter in the suburbs, none in the City. The private soldiers quartered in great houses lie upon the boards and have no beds and but a little if any firing, which is very hard this season. The General has sent to the City to provide bedding, or otherwise quarters to be provided for the soldiery in the City.

The Army Seizes Control

Wednesday, 6 December 1648—Pride's Purge bars members supporting the treaty with the King from entering the House of Commons

This day Colonel Rich's regiment of horse and Colonel Pride's foot were a guard to the Parliament and the City trained bands [i.e., militia] discharged.

Several members going to the House [in fact, around half the Commons by the time the purge was over] were seized upon and kept in custody by special order from the General and Council of the Army, which the House of Commons then sitting being informed of, it was ordered that the Sergeant at Arms attending the House of Commons should be required forthwith to go to the said members so seized and under a guard in the Queen's Court and Court of Wards and acquaint them that it is the pleasure of the House that they forthwith attend the service of the House. The Sergeant returning brought answer that the captain of the guard had order to secure them [i.e., the prisoners], which order he was to obey before any other command and therefore could not in prosecution thereof dismiss them till he had other orders to the contrary.

The Decision to Bring the King to Trial

Saturday, 23 December 1648—House of Commons

The House had much debate this day about bringing the great delinquents of the kingdom to speedy punishment and ordered a committee of thirty-eight to consider of drawing up a charge, and for that purpose to receive all informations and examinations of all witnesses for the matters of fact against the King and all other delinquents that may be thought fit to be brought to condign punishment.

The King is expected this night at Windsor Castle.

Thursday, 28 December 1648—the charge against the King

The committee appointed to consider of the drawing up of a charge against, and of the manner of the trial of, His Majesty reported an ordinance this day to the House for attainting him of High Treason and for trying him by such commissioners as should be nominated in the body of the said ordinance. The House having read it the first time ordered it to be read the second time tomorrow morning at 10 o'clock. The charge runs thus:

> That Charles Stuart hath acted contrary to his trust in departing from the Parliament, setting up his standard, making a war against them, and thereby [hath] been the occasion of

much bloodshed and misery to the people whom he was set over for good; that he gave commissions to Irish rebels, etc., and since was the occasion of a second war, etc., besides what he has done contrary to the liberties of the subject and tending to the destruction of the fundamental laws and liberties of this kingdom, etc.

Saturday, 30 December 1648—continued preparations for the King's trial

The House again had reported to them the Ordinance of Attainder and charge against the King (in the name of Charles Stuart) for High Treason, and ordered that the same should be committed to the former committee chosen for that business, who were to meet this afternoon and insert the names of such commissioners as should be appointed by the said ordinance for the trial of him. They were likewise to make some special provision in case the King should refuse to plead to the charge against him, and were to make report of the whole business on Monday morning next.

Monday, 1 January 1649

House of Commons

The ordinance for the King's trial is approved and forwarded to the House of Lords

This day (according to former order) the Commons had again reported to them the Ordinance of Attainder against the King in the name of Charles Stuart, and the names of such commissioners as should try him, consisting of lords, commons, officers of the Army, aldermen and other commanders of the City [of London], with some gentlemen from the counties, all of them consisting of one hundred fifty, and twenty of them are to be a committee [i.e., a quorum] for the trial of him and to give sentence against him. By this ordinance the commissioners are limited to a month's time to make a full determination of the business. The place of trial is not named in the ordi-

nance, so that whether it will be at Windsor or Westminster is not yet known. The ordinance is to be sent tomorrow to the House of Lords for their concurrence.

And to confirm the present trial and foundation thereof, and prevention of the like for the future, the House declared: Resolved, that the Lords and Commons in Parliament assembled do declare and adjudge that by the fundamental laws of this kingdom it is treason in the King of England for the time being to levy war against the Parliament and Kingdom of England.

Other actions by the House

The House ordered an ordinance to be brought in for enabling the commissioners of South Wales and Monmouth to proceed upon the sequestering of delinquents' estates in the said counties, and to remove obstructions therein.

A letter this day came from Mr. Elsynge, Clerk of the House of Commons, desiring the House by reason of his present indisposition to appoint a Clerk to attend them. The House hereupon voted that a committee should be appointed to send to Mr. Elsynge to take an account of him where the books and records of that House are, and to inventory the said books and records, and to present the names of fit and able persons that a sufficient Clerk may be elected out of them to be Clerk to the House. They likewise voted Mr. Phelps to be Clerk-Assistant to the House.

Other News

Theaters closed by the Army

The soldiers of the Army in the prosecution of an ordinance of Parliament secured all the players at Salisbury Court and Drury Lane, and brought them away prisoners in the midst of their acts, in their robes as then habited.

A private letter from Somerton calling for defensive associations against royalists and Presbyterians alike

Since the Parliament hath empowered us to raise forces and join ourselves in association with the Army and other well-affected people in the adjacent counties, we have not been altogether inactive in the said business but hope to bring it into such a speedy way as may be safe for this county—especially all the well-affected therein and those that join with us. Times may come, possibly, to put all the honest party of the kingdom to their shifts, and I could heartily wish that all other counties of the kingdom would begin betimes to provide for their own securities. When they do desire it, the opportunity being let slip, it may be too late. And surely if all the well-affected in each county would speedily strike into an association, it might be a great diversion of all our enemies' designs and give us hope of quietness and peace in this nation. And seeing that the Presbyterian ministers are to be frustrate in their intentions to enjoy pluralities [i.e., the holding of multiple church offices] and the tenth part of every man's estate [i.e., tithes], the people being left to a free choice of their minister and what minister, no doubt but they will endeavor (and we find it now their main design in this county) to preach down the power of God in his ministers, indeed, and to preach for forms of government and especially for their God (the continuance of tithes) of purpose to incense the people against this reformation, indeed both in Church and State, the benefit whereof our children's children will have cause to bless us for. And in respect likewise that the Grand Delinquent of the Kingdom, Charles Stuart, is to be brought to speedy justice (for which we have much cause to bless God) we shall find his party as active as the other. And though the Presbyters made but a seeming conjunction with their Brother Malignants for the carrying on of his traitorous interests, yet we fear you shall find them this next summer declaratively join with them for revenge of his army and all that have adhered to them. And therefore it is high time for all honest men in the several counties to associate betimes, before it be too late.

Tuesday, 2 January 1649

House of Lords

The Lords refuse to consent to the King's trial

The ordinance for trial of the King was by message this day carried up to the Lords for their concurrence. There sat many more lords this day in the House than usual of late, as the Earl of Northumberland, Earl of Manchester, Earl of Rutland, Lords North, Rochford, Maynard, Dacre, in all sixteen, the Earl of Denbigh Speaker. The Lords read the ordinance, but stuck much upon that declaratory vote: "The Lords and Commons do declare and adjudge that by the fundamental laws of this kingdom it is treason in the King of England for the time being to levy war against the Parliament and Kingdom of England, the Lords' concurrence to be desired." At last they agreed, as to a present answer to the Commons, that they would send answer by messengers of their own; and laying aside the business, adjourned until Thursday come seven-night.

Wednesday, 3 January 1649

House of Commons

The Commons proceed in the King's trial without the concurrence of the House of Lords

The House of Commons taking notice that the Lords had ejected their ordinance for trial of the King and adjourned for a week, they first passed instructions for some of their members to go up to examine the Lords' journal-book concerning their declaration and ordinance that was the day before sent up for trial of the King. And at their return they brought to the House three votes which their lordships had made: (1) to send answers by messengers of their own; (2) that their lordships do not concur to the declaration; and (3) that their lordships rejected the ordinance for the trial of the King.

Hereupon the Commons voted that all members of the House of Commons, and others, appointed by order of that House or ordinance of both Houses of Parliament to act in any ordinance wherein the Lords are joined, be empowered and enjoined to sit, act, and execute in the said several committees of themselves, notwithstanding the House of Peers join not with them herein.

They then also ordered an expedient to be brought concerning the King, the substance like the former ordinance for his trial, [but] with the foregoing declaration intended for both Houses now to be by the Commons only. The committee to sit presently and to report it this afternoon, during which time of that committee's sitting the House adjourned.

Afterwards the House sat again and the ordinance was reported by the said committee according to the instructions which were made, and recommitted back again to the said committee and ordered to be brought in again the next day. The six lords [i.e., the lords mentioned in the original ordinance] to be left out in this and also the three judges. Serjeant Bradshaw, Serjeant Nicholas, etc., to be put in, and Mr. Steel and others to be assistants.

Mr. Speaker acquainted the House with a letter he had received by the French Ambassador from the Queen of England out of France. The letter upon debate was laid aside and not read.

The Army

Urgent need to collect taxes to pay the Army

A letter was sent by His Excellency the Lord Fairfax to the several counties hereafter named about their assessments for the Army, as followeth:

Gentlemen,
I desire you would cause the arrears of the assessments for the Army that is in your counties to be forthwith brought

Lord Fairfax: Lord Fairfax suffered the fate of moderate revolutionaries—he was overtaken by the very revolution he helped create. A brilliant and courageous soldier often wounded in Parliament's service, his battlefield victories gained him the title of commander-in-chief of the Army in 1647. But Fairfax's abilities were unequal to the tricky political infighting that followed the ending of the Civil War, as radicals pressed for extreme measures to be taken against the King. Socially conservative, he envisioned an England ruled by people of his class under the nominal leadership of a limited monarchy. He stood on the sidelines during Pride's Purge and kept a low profile during the trial, refusing to sit as one of the King's judges and perhaps intervening behind the scenes to prevent his execution. To Fairfax and many of his fellow officers, it was one thing to fight the King and quite another to open the floodgates of social anarchy by abolishing the monarchy altogether. He resigned his command in 1650 and later broke with Cromwell. He was part of the delegation sent in 1660 to invite Charles II to return to England and was granted a royal pardon. Fairfax County, Virginia, takes its name from his family. Miniature by John Hoskins, 1650. Reproduced by kind permission of the Trustees of the Leeds Castle Foundation, Maidstone.

unto your treasurers, and the last six months assessed, levied, collected, and brought in as aforesaid, to the end it may be ready to supply that regiment who shall have your county for its assignations of pay by order and warrant from the committee of Lords and Commons for the Army which you shall have very suddenly. This being performed, I shall take care that the heavy burden of free quarter shall be removed from all those who shall duly pay in their assessments. Expecting your performance hereof, I remain

Your very assured friend,
T. Fairfax

Queen Street
January 2, 1649

This letter was sent to the committees of the several counties hereunder named: Kent, Surrey, Berkshire, Buckinghamshire, Hertford, Bedford, Huntingdon, Cambridge, Suffolk, Norfolk, Essex, Middlesex, Sussex, Hampshire, Wiltshire, Northamptonshire, Leicestershire, Warwick.

Thursday, 4 January 1649

House of Commons

The House declares itself to be the supreme power in England

The House this day (as was appointed) had the ordinance for the trial of the King by the name of Charles Stuart reported with some amendments. And in respect the House of Lords had rejected it, they ordered the House should be turned into a grand committee to consider of the power of the Commons of England when assembled in Parliament. In fine, the committee came to this resolution, that it should be reported to the House these votes following as the opinion of the said committee:

Resolved, that the Commons of England in Parliament assembled do declare that the people are, under God, the original of all just power; and do also declare that the Commons of England in Parliament assembled, being chosen by and representing the people, have the supreme power in this nation; and do also declare that whatsoever is enacted or declared for law by the Commons in Parliament assembled hath the force of law, and all the people of this nation are included thereby, although the consent and concurrence of King or House of Peers be not had thereunto.

These being reported to the House, the House put them one after another to the question and there was not one negative voice to any one of them. Then an ordinance for trial of Charles Stuart was again read and assented unto, and ordered to be forthwith engrossed in parchment and to be brought in tomorrow morning.

The House ordered that the Clerk of that House should be enjoined not to give out any copy of the said ordinance for trial of Charles Stuart, either to any member of the House or any other whatsoever.

Friday, 5 January 1649

House of Commons

From the Journals of the House of Commons

Ordered, that the General [Lord Fairfax] be sent to and desired to take order to prohibit all delinquents and Papists from coming to or staying in the City of London or the liberties [i.e., district] thereof, or within the late lines of communication, or within ten miles of the City of London; and to secure the persons of such as shall be found within the limits aforesaid six days after the date hereof, except such persons as shall be licensed under the hands of Mr. Francis Allen and Mr. Samuel Moyer to come to prosecute their compositions with effect [i.e., complete their surrender], or such as have already compounded for their delinquency and have paid in their money according to orders and directions of Parliament given in that behalf.

Ordered, that a book of vellum be forthwith prepared for entering all the public acts of this House; and that all the public acts of this House be entered in the said book accordingly.

Ordered, that the ordinance touching the erecting of an High Court of Justice for trial of the King be engrossed and brought in tomorrow morning the first business.

Ordered, that Mr. Humphrey Edwards and Mr. Fry do repair to Mr. Prynne and show him the scandalous book or pamphlet entitled *A Brief Memento to the Present Unparliamentary Junto, Touching their Present Intentions and Proceedings to Depose and Execute Charles Stuart, their Lawful King,* and to know of him if he will own and avow the said book.

Ordered, that the Lord General be desired to command his Marshal to put the ordinance of 28 September 1647 concerning scandalous pamphlets in execution.

Resolved, that Henry Scobell, Esq., be and is hereby nominated and appointed Clerk of this House, in the place and stead of Henry Elsynge, Esq. And it is further ordered that the patent of the said Henry Elsynge be called in and that Mr. Scobell do sign the orders and proceedings of this House.

Saturday, 6 January 1649

House of Commons

The House passes the act for the King's trial

The ordinance of Parliament for trying of the King was this day brought in fairly engrossed in parchment according to former order, and was read and assented unto. The manner of his trial as before; the time and place, whether at London or Windsor, nothing further, but that is left to the commissioners who are to try him, and they are to meet on Monday next in the Painted Chamber, Westminster, and to proceed in order as to the trial, which they are to go on withal without intermission.

Other actions by the House

A letter came from the Committee of Estates in Scotland resident here, laying open and pressing much for unity of councils and actions according to the covenants betwixt the two kingdoms, desiring that the House would not proceed to try or execute the King till the advice of that nation be had, thereunto the Parliament of Scotland sat down last Thursday the fourth instant. We will not presage anything of their proceedings until it discover itself. The Scots' letter was not read, but ordered to be considered of another time.

The House had much debate concerning proceeding of law, the issuing of writs and the like, in what name they should now be made in relation that King and Lords are laid aside. The House referred it to a committee to draw up an expedient and report it to the House with speed.

Text of the Act Ordering the King's Trial

An Act of the Commons of England Assembled in Parliament for Erecting of an High Court of Justice for the Trying and Judging of Charles Stuart, King of England

Whereas it is notorious that Charles Stuart, the now King of England, not content with those many encroachments which his predecessors had made upon the people in their rights and freedoms, hath had a wicked design totally to subvert the ancient and fundamental laws and liberties of this nation, and in their place to introduce an arbitrary and tyrannical government, and that besides all other evil ways and means to bring this design to pass he hath prosecuted it with fire and sword, levied and maintained a cruel war in the land against the Parliament and kingdom, whereby the country hath been miserably wasted, the public treasure exhausted, trade decayed, thousands of people murdered, and infinite other mischiefs committed, for all which high and treasonable offenses the said Charles Stuart might long since justly have been brought to exemplary and condign punishment; whereas also the Parliament, well hoping that the restraint and imprisonment of his person (after it had pleased God to deliver him into their hands) would have quieted the

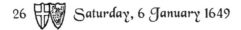

distempers of the kingdom, did forbear to proceed judicially against him, but found by sad experience that such their remissness served only to encourage him and his accomplices in the continuance of their evil practices and in raising of new commotions, rebellions and invasions; for prevention, therefore, of the like or greater inconveniences, and to the end no chief officer or magistrate whatsoever may hereafter presume traitorously and maliciously to imagine or contrive the enslaving or destroying of the English Nation and to expect impunity for so doing, be it ordained and enacted by the Commons in Parliament, and it is hereby ordained and enacted by authority thereof, that Thomas, Lord Fairfax, Oliver Cromwell, Henry Ireton . . . [one hundred thirty-five commissioners are listed in all, consisting mainly of members of the Commons and Army officers] shall be, and are hereby appointed and required to be, commissioners and judges for the hearing, trying and adjudging of the said Charles Stuart. And the said commissioners, or any twenty or more of them, shall be and are hereby authorized and constituted an High Court of Justice to meet and sit at such convenient time and place as by the said commissioners or the major part of twenty or more of them under their hands and seals shall be appointed and notified by public proclamation in the Great Hall or Palace Yard at Westminster; and to adjourn from time to time and from place to place as the said High Court or major part thereof meeting shall hold fit; and to take order for the charging of him, the said Charles Stuart, with the crimes and treasons above-mentioned; and for the receiving of his personal answer thereunto; and for the examination of witnesses upon oath (which the court hath hereby authority to administer) or otherwise, and taking any other evidence concerning the same; and thereupon, or in default of such answer, to proceed to final sentence according to justice and the merit of the cause; and such final sentence to execute or cause to be executed speedily and impartially. And the said court is hereby authorized and required to appoint and direct all such officers, attendants and other circumstances as they or the major part of them shall in any sort judge necessary or useful for the orderly and good managing of the premises. And Thomas, Lord Fairfax, the General, and all officers and soldiers under his command, and all officers of justice and other well-affected persons, are hereby authorized and required to be aiding and assisting unto the said court in the due execution of the trust hereby committed, pro-

vided that this act and the authority hereby granted do continue in force for the space of one month from the making hereof, and no longer.

Henry Scobell
Clerk of the House of Commons

Other News

The City of London given five days to raise £19,000

The Common Council of London this day agreed upon an order to be published in all churches tomorrow about the assessments of the Army:

> Whereas the sum of £19,000 (being a fortnight's pay for the
> forces under the command of His Excellency the Lord
> Fairfax) is required to be paid out of the arrears of the four
> former assessments on or before Wednesday next, or else that
> the whole Army must of necessity be quartered in the City of
> London, for prevention whereof a committee by order of the
> Common Council made their address unto the Committee of
> the Army, with a desire that the said committee would be
> pleased to forbear the quartering of soldiers in the City until
> that day or such further time as might be obtained, in which
> time the said £19,000 shall be paid. To which the Committee
> of the Army returned answer that if they shall not under-
> stand upon Thursday next that the said money shall be paid
> to the relief of the said forces on Friday next, or then receive
> the names of those which are in arrears upon the said assess-
> ments, that then they shall be forced to quarter the whole
> Army within this City on Saturday next, and especially on
> them that are in arrears. Wherefore for the better avoiding of
> inconveniences and danger to the City, it is the desire of this
> Court and Common Council that the several ministers of this
> City will tomorrow in the forenoon and afternoon openly
> publish this unto the congregations and effectually move and
> stir up the people to pay their money in arrears for the said

Army on Monday next, wherein the said £19,000 may be furnished as is required.

The "Agreement of the People" discussed by the Army

This day the General Council of Officers heard the whole report of the officers appointed to propose what particulars of the "Agreement of the People" were fundamental or essential and what not, and passed a declaration or form of subscription to the Agreement. The alterations are to be propounded to the Council on Monday next, and then the whole Agreement will be finished and accordingly subscribed.

Monday, 8 January 1649

House of Commons

From the Journals of the House of Commons

Resolved, that the endorsement upon the act for erecting an High Court of Justice for trial of the King be in these words following: "6 January 1649. Read the third time, and upon the question: Resolved, that it be enacted for law and have the force of a law, and that the Clerk do endorse the same accordingly."

Ordered, that tomorrow morning at 9 o'clock this House be resolved into a grand committee to take into consideration the business concerning the government and settlement of the kingdom; and that Mr. Speaker do put the House in mind hereof; and that the members of this House be desired then to give their attendance here.

High Court of Justice

The court begins to organize itself—meeting in the Painted Chamber at Westminster, fifty-three commissioners present, as reported in the Journal kept by John Phelps, Clerk of the Court

The commissioners met on Monday, the eighth day of January, 1649, in the Painted Chamber at Westminster, where the act [establishing the court] was openly read and the court called.

The commissioners of the court being as aforesaid met, and informing themselves of the tenor of their commission, they accordingly appoint the said court to be holden in the same place on Wednesday, the tenth of the said month of January, and ordered proclamation thereof to be made in the Great Hall at Westminster by Edward Dendy, Sergeant at Arms, authorizing him thereunto by precept under their hands and seals, in these words following:

By virtue of an Act of the Commons of England Assembled in Parliament for Erecting of an High Court of Justice for the Trying and Judging of Charles Stuart, King of England, we whose names are hereunder written (being commissioners, amongst others, nominated in the said act) do hereby appoint that the High Court of Justice mentioned in the said act shall be holden in the Painted Chamber in the Palace of Westminster on Wednesday, the tenth day of this instant January, by 1 of the clock in the afternoon, and this we do appoint to be notified by public proclaiming hereof in the Great Hall at Westminster tomorrow, being the ninth day of this instant January, betwixt the hours of nine and eleven in the forenoon. In testimony whereof we have hereunto set our hands and seals this eighth day of January, anno Domini 1649 [signed by thirty-seven commissioners].

And in order to the more regular and due proceedings of the said court, they nominate officers and accordingly choose Mr. Aske, Dr. Dorislaus, Mr. Steel, and Mr. Cook [to be] Counsel to attend the said court; Mr. Greaves and Mr. John Phelps [to be] Clerks, to whom notice thereof was ordered to be given. Mr. Edward Walford, Mr. John Powell, Mr. John King, Mr. Phineas Payne, and Mr. Hull are chosen Messengers to attend this court.

Sala Regalis cum Curia West-monasterij vulgo Westminster hall

Tuesday, 9 January 1649

House of Lords

The Lords discuss their refusal to consent to the King's trial

Their lordships had in debate their last votes about trial of the King and that something should be published to satisfy upon what grounds they rejected the commission for trial of the King, but came to no resolution herein. They have sat this week but done nothing we hear of.

House of Commons

The King's trial is proclaimed

This morning (according to order of the commissioners for trial of the King yesterday) proclamation was made in Westminster Hall to give notice that the commissioners were to sit again tomorrow and that all who had anything to say against the King might then be heard. This proclamation was in this manner made: Sergeant Dendy, Sergeant at Arms to the commissioners, rode into Westminster Hall with the Mace belonging to the House of Commons on his shoulders, and some officers also attending him all bare[headed] and six trumpeters on horseback, a guard of horse and foot attending in the Palace Yard. The trumpeters sounded in the middle of the hall and the drums beat in the Palace Yard, and proclamation was made as aforesaid.

Westminster Hall and New Palace Yard: Westminster Hall, to the left, was one of the largest buildings in England and the center of its legal system. On 9 January, Sergeant Dendy entered the hall on horseback to proclaim the High Court's formal creation while his escort of soldiers remained outside. On the afternoon of 20 January, the great north doors would again be thrown open, admitting spectators to the first day of the trial. The hours of the court's sitting were marked by a bell in the fourteenth-century clock tower located across New Palace Yard, not far from where Big Ben rings today. The neighborhood was full of taverns and coffee houses, including an establishment nicknamed "Hell," where the objects of Pride's Purge were temporarily held. Engraving by Wenceslaus Hollar, 1647. From the Art Collection of the Folger Shakespeare Library. Reproduced by kind permission.

The House of Commons then sitting ordered that Sergeant Dendy should forthwith make the same proclamation about the trial of the King and in the same manner at the Old Exchange and in Cheapside, London, which was accordingly done.

Exclusion of the King and House of Lords necessitates an alteration of judicial procedures

The House this day had much debate [about] what alteration of proceedings should be made in courts of justice now that the King and Lords were to be laid aside, and whether all writs should run in the name of one person (as formerly "Charles, by the Grace of God, etc.") or not. At last they came to this result, that the name of any one particular person should not be inserted as the style of any common writ or otherwise for the time to come, and that it should be referred to a committee for settling proceedings in courts of justice to consider how and in what manner the style should be hereafter.

They likewise voted that this present Great Seal of England should be broken in pieces and that a new one should be forthwith made; yet in the meantime all proceedings under the Great Seal to be good till the new one be confirmed.

They considered what should be engraved on the said new Great Seal, and ordered that the Arms of England, the Harp, and the Arms of Ireland should be engraved on one side of the said seal; that the inscription on that side [of] the seal should be "The Great Seal of England"; that the inscription on the other side of the said seal, where the sculpture or map of the Parliament is to be engraved, shall be these words "In the First Year of Freedom by God's Blessing Restored, 1649."

The Army

Typical petition presented to Lord Fairfax urging the punishment of the King and his followers and the radical reformation of government along lines laid down in the Levellers' "Humble Petition" (September 1648) and the Army's "Remonstrance" (November 1648)

The humble petition of the officers and soldiers, together with divers of the well-affected inhabitants in the Isle of Wight, Ports-

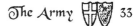

mouth, and Hurst showeth: that our equal sensibleness (with our fellow soldiers and countrymen) of the overflowing miseries and insup-
portable grievances by the war brought (and subject to be continued)
upon the people by common enemies and apostates, also our sad
apprehensions of the late dismal and delusive treaty with a dangerous, political and conquered enemy, and our earnest love to righteousness, peace and union upon just principles, doth invite us to
declare our sincere affection to, and approbation of, the just and
reasonable desires mentioned in the large petition of September 11
last, with the petitions of divers counties and that seasonable
Remonstrance of Your Excellency and Council in conjunction with the
said large petition. And calling to mind the manifold dispensations of
God to this nation by the continued successes given to the unwearied
labors of Your Excellency and the Army under your command
against the enemies of our peace in the first and second war [i.e., the
two phases of the Civil War, 1642-46 and 1648], together with the present enforced and necessary undertaking in behalf of all the faithful
and cordial people of this nation which hath freely adventured their
lives and all that was dear to them in the common cause of public
good, it encourageth us to believe that the same God which hath
blessed you in the former will also crown these your honorable
endeavors with happy success in the latter.

Wherefore we humbly desire that Your Excellency and Council
will still manifest your constant and sincere affections in pursuance of
justice to a righteous settlement [and] (by vigorous and speedy act-
ings) not leave place for yourselves to be diverted from those your
declared resolutions, but singly and impartially proceed so that the
great disturbers of this nation's peace may either be cleared of those
great and heinous crimes publicly declared and laid to their charge,
or else condemned according to principles of law and justice; and that
such only for the future may be employed in any places of office and
trust in the Commonwealth as are of known fidelity to the public
interest, [that] the heavy burdens of the wearied people may with all
convenient speed be removed, and that after the great expense of
blood and treasure the nation may enjoy that long-desired issue of a
firm and lasting peace. For the speedy accomplishment whereof, we
do and shall (in the strength of God, with all readiness and cheerful-
ness) engage our lives and all that is dear unto us with Your
Excellency and all others who shall join with you herein, being will-

ing to cast our whole might into that common treasury for the obtaining of so reasonable and just ends aforementioned.

Subscribed by above 1,600 persons and presented to His Excellency by Lieutenant Cuppage, Lieutenant Ward, Ensign Fox, Marshal Templer, and Mr. Darnford, Master Gunner of Plymouth.

Wednesday, 10 January 1649

House of Commons

Arrest of William Prynne ordered

The House this day considered of Mr. Prynne's answer returned by two Members of Parliament Friday last (concerning the pamphlet entitled *A Brief Memento* to which his name was [attached], whether he would own it or not) which was to this purpose, that when he should be sent unto in a legal way and by a sufficient authority to be resolved therein, he would answer them as should be desired. The House hereupon ordered that Mr. Prynne by this answer doth deny the supreme authority of this kingdom; that the Sergeant at Arms should be required forthwith to take the said Mr. Prynne into custody till further order.

Ordinance for altering judicial procedures recommitted

The committee appointed to consider of settling proceedings in courts of justice again made report thereof this day to the House, who read an ordinance to this purpose before the second time, and upon the question recommitted it. And because the commissioners concerning the King's trial were to sit at 2 of the clock this afternoon, the House adjourned till tomorrow morning.

High Court of Justice

Preparations for the King's trial continue—meeting in the Painted Chamber, forty-five commissioners present

The commissioners for the trial of the King met accordingly this afternoon in the Painted Chamber. They then nominated Serjeant Bradshaw to be President of the Court, Mr. Steel was chosen Attorney General, Mr. Cook, Solicitor; and these, with Dr. Dorislaus and Mr. Aske, to draw up and manage the charge against the King. Some other officers to the court were then nominated, after which proclamation was made to proclaim the court, and the commissioners called and those present notified by the President. Then Sergeant Dendy was called to give an account that he had caused the proclamation to be made according to order, which he did. And then the court adjourned till Friday 2 o'clock to meet again in the Painted Chamber. The place for trial of the King is not yet declared.

Thursday, 11 January 1649

House of Commons

Miscellaneous business

The House of Commons this day spent much time in debating an ordinance for settling and regulating the affairs of the Navy which was read a second time and committed.

The House was informed that the Sergeant's man that served the warrant of the House on Mr. Prynne, to take him into the custody of the Sergeant at Arms, was at the door. He was called in and acquainted the House that after he had served Mr. Prynne with the said warrant, he [i.e., Prynne] told him that as he was coming to the House to perform his duty therein for the county for which he was elected, he was apprehended by Sir Hardress Waller and Colonel Pride and secured as [a] prisoner ever since; that being not discharged of that imprisonment, he could not submit to that order which he had for any other restraint to be laid upon him, and therefore he refused to obey the same.

The House then ordered that the answer of the General Council of the Army should be read concerning the secluded and secured [i.e., excluded and imprisoned] members; the House debated much upon

John Bradshaw: When named to the presidency of the High Court on 10 January, John Bradshaw had awesome responsibilities, if not greatness, suddenly thrust upon him. As the trial was first conceived, the three greatest judicial figures of the land were to preside over it: the Lord Chief Justice of England, the Lord Chief Justice of the Common Pleas, and the Lord Chief Baron of the Exchequer. But when all three refused to serve, the court had to make do with Bradshaw, a provincial judge known for his republican sympathies. Hardly anyone considered him a legal luminary, but even though he was upstaged by the King at every turn and his rambling speeches fell short of eloquence, he nonetheless managed to express his vision of popular sovereignty and of government subject to the rule of law. He wore scarlet robes for the sentencing, and, as presiding judge, he was the first to sign the death warrant. He died ten years later, on the eve of the Restoration. Detail from a double portrait, attributed to Peter Lely, of the Regicides John Bradshaw and Hugh Peters. Reproduced by kind permission of The Lord Tollemache, Helmingham Hall. Photo by courtesy of the Courtauld Institute of Art.

this business and ordered that they approve of the substance of the said answer.

The House then appointed a committee to consider what was fit to be done further upon the said answer, who were to report with all speed, and Mr. Prynne's cause [will be] more particularly debated Saturday next.

Friday, 12 January 1649

High Court of Justice

The court installs its President and settles its procedures—meeting in the Painted Chamber, thirty-three commissioners "with divers more" present, as reported in the Journal kept by John Phelps, Clerk of the Court

Serjeant Bradshaw upon special summons attended this court, being one of the commissioners thereof, and being according to former order called to take his place of President of the said court, made an earnest apology for himself to be excused. But therein not prevailing, in obedience to the commands and desires of this court, he submitted to their order and took place accordingly. And thereupon the said court ordered concerning him as followeth: that John Bradshaw, Serjeant at Law, who is appointed President of this court, should be called by the name and have the title of Lord President, and that as well without as within the said court during the commission and sitting of the said court, against which title he pressed much to be heard to offer his exceptions but was therein overruled by the court.

Mr. Andrew Broughton attended according to former order, and it was thereupon again ordered that Andrew Broughton and John Phelps, Gent., be and they are hereby constituted Clerks of the said court and enjoined to give their attendance from time to time accordingly.

Ordered, that the Counsel assigned (or such as they or any of them shall appoint) shall have power to search for all records and writings concerning the King's trial, and to take into their custody or order the producing of all such records and papers or copies thereof by any clerk or other person whatsoever at or before the said trial as they shall judge requisite, the said Counsel giving a note under their hands of their receipt of all such original books and papers which they shall so take into their custody. And that the said Counsel shall have power to send for such person or persons at or before the said trial and to appoint by writing under their hands their attendance for the service of the state in this business as they shall think requisite, requiring all persons concerned to yield obedience thereunto at their perils.

Sir Hardress Waller, Knight, and Colonel Harrison are ordered to desire the Lord General from time to time to appoint sufficient guards to attend and guard the said court during their sitting.

Ordered, that Colonel Tichborne, Colonel Rowe, Mr. Blakiston, and Mr. Fry, members of this court, shall and do make preparations for the trial of the King that it may be performed in a solemn manner, and that they take care for other necessary provisions and accommodations in and about that trial, and are to appoint and command such workmen in and to their assistance as they shall think fit.

Mr. Love reporteth from the committee appointed January tenth instant to consider of the circumstances in matters of order for trial of the King. And it is thereupon ordered that in managing the proceedings in open court at the time of the King's trial none of the court do speak but the President and Counsel, and in case of any difficulty arising to anyone, that he speak not to the matter openly but desire the President that the court may please to advise. By which order it is not intended that any of the commissioners be debarred at the examination of any witness to move the Lord President to propound such question to the witness as shall be thought meet for the better disquisition and finding out of the truth.

Ordered, that there shall be a Marshal to attend this court if there be cause.

Ordered, that the Lord President and Counsel do manage the trial against the King according to instructions to be given them by the court, and that the committee for considering of all circumstances for the managing of the King's trial do consider of rules and instructions in that behalf, and are to consult with the Counsel and address themselves to the Lord President for advice in the premises.

Ordered, that the Counsel do bring in the charge against the King on Monday next.

The committee for considering of the circumstances of order for the King's trial, together with Sir Hardress Waller, Colonel Whalley, Mr. Scot, Colonel Tichborne, Colonel Harrison, Lieutenant General Cromwell, and Colonel Deane, are appointed to consider of the place for trying the King and make report tomorrow in the afternoon, and are to meet tomorrow morning in the Inner Court of Wards at 9 of the clock, and who else of the court please may be there.

The court adjourned itself till the morrow in the afternoon at 2 of the clock.

Saturday, 13 January 1649

High Court of Justice

Private meeting in the Painted Chamber, thirty-eight commissioners present, as reported in Phelps's Journal

The court, being to make further preparations for the King's trial, sit private. The Sergeant at Arms is authorized to employ such other messengers as shall be needful for the service of the court, giving in their names to the Clerks of this Court.

Ordered, that the Sergeant at Arms do search and secure the vaults under the Painted Chamber, taking such assistance therein from the soldiery as shall be needful.

Mr. Garland reporteth from the committee for considering of the place for the King's trial. And the court thereupon ordered that the said trial of the King shall be in Westminster Hall; that the place for the King's trial shall be where the Courts of King's Bench and Chancery sit in Westminster Hall; and that the partitions between the said two courts be therefore taken down; and that the committee for making preparations for the King's trial are to take care thereof accordingly.

The court adjourned itself till Monday at 2 of the clock in the afternoon to this place.

Monday, 15 January 1649

House of Commons

Miscellaneous actions concerning the King's trial

The House ordered £1,000 to be forthwith paid out of the Revenue for defraying some incident charges concerning the trial of the King.

A petition was presented by a committee from the Commons of the City of London in Common Council assembled. The petition was to desire that the House would proceed in execution of justice against all grand and capital actors in the late war against the Parliament, from the highest to the lowest; that the Militia, Navy, and places of power be in faithful hands; for recovery and increase of the trade of the City; to endeavor the settling of the votes (of their [i.e., the House's] declaration that the supreme power is in them) upon foundations of righteousness and peace, resolving to stand by them to the utmost.

High Court of Justice

The court meets again privately to consider the charge against the King, fifty-eight commissioners present

The High Court of Justice concerning the trial of the King sat this day, heard his charge read, which was very long, and therefore ordered a committee to abbreviate it and to peruse the proofs upon the matters of fact thereof and to report all on Wednesday next at 8 o'clock in the morning. They ordered that the Parliament should be moved to put off the next term [i.e., session of the law courts] for fourteen days longer in respect of this trial, in order whereunto they are making the Courts of King's Bench and Chancery into one place of judicature for the better accommodation of His Majesty and the commissioners.

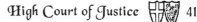

Tuesday, 16 January 1649

House of Commons

Miscellaneous actions

This day the House passed an act for the adjournment of the next term for fourteen days.

They had some debate about papers sent from Scotland directed to "William Lenthall, Esq., Speaker of the House of Commons" and no more, whereas they used to add "to be communicated to the House of Commons," by this acknowledging them a House. And so the House thought not fit to read them.

Other News

The Scots object to the proceedings of the English Parliament

From Scotland the letters say the Parliament began there on January the fourth, some three or four days before. The Wednesday following was observed as a Day of Humiliation, and the proceedings of the Parliament of England being reported, it was taken into deep consideration and the whole Parliament in general (no man contradicting it) did dissent from the proceedings of the Parliament of England: (1) in the toleration of religion in order to the Covenant; (2) in the trial of the King; (3) in alteration of the form of government.

Wednesday, 17 January 1649

High Court of Justice

Details settled for the conduct of the trial—meeting in the Painted Chamber, fifty-six commissioners present, as reported in Phelps's Journal

Three proclamations made and all parties concerned are required to give attendance.

Ordered, that the commissioners of this court who have not hitherto appeared be summoned by warrants under the hands of the Clerks of this Court to give their personal attendance at this court to perform the service to which they are by act of the Commons of England assembled in Parliament appointed and required.

Ordered, that the Sergeant at Arms attending this court or his deputy do forthwith summon all the aforesaid commissioners making default who reside or dwell within twenty miles of London. Particular warrants to every one of them were accordingly issued forth for their attendance.

Upon report made by Colonel Hutchinson from the committee to consider of the manner of bringing the King to trial, the court order as followeth: Ordered, that Sir Robert Cotton's house be the place where the King shall lodge during his trial; that the chamber in Sir Robert Cotton's house next the study, there shall be the King's bedchamber; that the great chamber before the said lodging chamber be for the King's dining room, and that a guard consisting of thirty officers and other choice men do always attend the King, who are to attend him at his lodging above stairs, and that two of the said thirty do always attend in his bedchamber; that place for a court guard of two hundred foot soldiers be built in Sir Robert Cotton's garden near the waterside; that ten companies of foot be constantly upon the guard for securing Sir Robert Cotton's house, and those companies to be quartered in the Court of Requests, the Painted Chamber, and other necessary places thereabouts; that the passage that cometh out of the Old Palace into Westminster Hall be made up at the entrance of the said passage next the said guard; that the top of the stairs at the Court of Wards' door have a crossbar made to it; that the King be brought out of Sir Robert Cotton's house to his trial the lower way into Westminster Hall, and so brought to the Bar in the face of the court, attended by the above-said guard above stairs; that two rails of about forty foot distance from the place where the court shall sit in Westminster Hall be made cross the said hall, for the effectual and substantial doing whereof this court do refer it to the care of the committee appointed to consider of the manner of bringing the King to trial, who are likewise to take care for raising the floor in such part of the hall as they shall think fit for placing of the guards, and that a rail or rails from the court down to the hall gate be made in such manner as they shall think fit on the [Court of] Common Pleas' side to keep the people from the soldiers; that there be guards set upon the leads and other places that have windows to look into the hall; that the General be desired from time to time to send and appoint convenient guards of horse for the convenient sitting of the court; that twenty officers or other gentlemen do attend upon the Lord President from time to time, to and from this court through Westminster Hall; that the Officers of the Ordnance do send unto this court two hundred halberds or partizans lying within the Tower of London for the arming of the guards that are to attend this court; that at the time of the trial of the King the commissioners do, before their sitting in the court, meet in the Exchequer Chamber and do from thence come up the hall into the court; that all back doors from the house called Hell [an abutting tavern] be stopped up during the King's trial; that lodgings be prepared for the Lord President at Sir Abraham Williams's house in the New Palace Yard during the sitting of this court, and that all provisions and necessaries be provided for his lordship; that Sir Henry Mildmay, Mr. Holland and Mr. Edwards do take care for providing all provisions and necessaries for the King during his trial; that Sir Henry Mildmay, Mr. Holland and Mr. Edwards do likewise take care for all necessaries for the Lord President.

Ordered, that the committee for considering of the manner of bringing the King to trial do consider what habits [i.e., gowns] the officers of this court shall have, who are to advise with some heralds-at-arms therein and concerning the ordering [i.e., ceremonial protocol] of the said officers; that a Sword be carried before the Lord President at the trial of the King; that John Humphreys, Esq., do bear the Sword before the Lord President; that a Mace or Maces together with a Sword be likewise carried before the Lord President.

This court doth adjourn itself to 3 of the clock in the afternoon.

The court reconvenes—afternoon meeting as reported in Phelps's Journal

Three proclamations. The court is cleared of strangers and they sit private.

The charge against the King is presented by the Counsel and ordered to be recommitted to the committee appointed for advice

Bradshaw's Hat: Throughout the trial there were worries that an attempt might be made to rescue the King or harm his judges. Guards were posted on roofs and stairs, cellars were searched for bombs, and the area around Westminster Hall was placed under constant armed surveillance. As a further precaution, the Lord President wore this steel-lined beaver. Department of Antiquities, Ashmolean Museum, Oxford. Reproduced by kind permission.

with the Counsel concerning the charge against the King, who are to contract the same and fit it for the court's proceeding thereupon according to the act of Parliament in that behalf. And the same committee are likewise to take care for the King's coming to Westminster to trial at such time as to them shall seem meet, and Lieutenant General Cromwell is added to the said committee, and the Counsel are to attend this court with the said charge tomorrow at 2 of the clock in the afternoon. And thereupon: Ordered, that the committee for considering of the manner of bringing the King to trial do meet tomorrow morning at 8 of the clock in the Exchequer Chamber.

The court adjourned itself till the morrow at 2 of the clock in the afternoon, to the same place.

Thursday, 18 January 1649

House of Commons

The House reaffirms that it is the supreme power in England

A message this day came from the Lords which was grounded upon the dissent of the Lords' Commissioners of the Great Seal joined with the Commons' that they could not agree to pass the act of the Commons for adjourning the term without the Lords' concurrence was had thereto, and that by the instructions given to the said commissioners, the Commons' Commissioners could do nothing without assent of one of them [i.e., one of the Lords' Commissioners]. Their lordships therefore sent down a message to the Commons desiring their concurrence to an ordinance for adjourning the term for a fortnight, and that the Commissioners of the Great Seal of England may be required to pass the same under the Great Seal of England.

The Commons having formerly declared that the supreme power of England is vested only in the people and their representatives, and therefore voted that all committees which before consisted of Lords and Commons should have power to act to all intents and purposes though the Lords join not herein, the question was put whether they should adhere to their former votes and decline the power of their lordships, or else own the Lords as formerly by agreeing with them in this ordinance. This held much debate in the House, and at last the question was put whether the House would concur with their lordships herein. And it was resolved by the Commons assembled in Parliament that the House would not agree with their lordships herein, but would send answer by messengers of their own.

These two businesses was the debate of the whole day.

High Court of Justice

The chief prosecutor excuses himself—private meeting in the Exchequer Chamber at Westminster, thirty-seven commissioners present, as reported in Phelps's Journal

Westminster in the Mid-Seventeenth Century: The long narrow building at A is Westminster Hall. Westminster Abbey is to its left. Among the buildings abutting the hall on the river side are the House of Commons and Sir Robert Cotton's house, where the King resided during the trial. During days when he was not in court, Charles was held in St. James's Palace, at B. It was from there that on the morning of 30 January he walked across the park to Whitehall. The scaffold would have been located at C, in the street in front of the Banqueting House. Charing Cross, at D, is where several signers of the King's death warrant were themselves executed in 1660. Detail from Richard Newcourt's 1658 map of London and Westminster. By permission of the British Library. The labels A, B, C, and D have been added.

Here the court sit private.

Colonel Tichborne, one of the commissioners of this court, informeth the court that he was with Mr. Steel, Attorney of this court, and found him in his bed very sick and by reason thereof not like to attend (as yet) the service of this court according to former order, and desired him (the said Colonel) to signify that he (the said Mr. Steel)

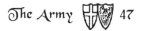

no way declineth the service of the said court out of any disaffection to it, but professeth himself to be so clear in the business that if it should please God to restore him he should manifest his good affection to the said cause, and that it is an addition to his affliction that he cannot attend this court to do that service that they have expected from him and as he desires to perform.

The court adjourned itself till tomorrow 2 of the clock in the afternoon.

Other News

A Member of Parliament imprisoned during Pride's Purge escapes

This evening Major General Massey, one of the secluded members, made his escape from St. James's where he was prisoner.

Friday, 19 January 1649

High Court of Justice

Final preparations for the King's trial—private meeting in the Painted Chamber, forty-eight commissioners present

The High Court of Justice for trial of the King this day met after the rising of the House in the Painted Chamber and heard the proof to the several Articles of Impeachment against the King, who this day was brought from Windsor to St. James's, where he lodged this night.

The Army

One petition signed and another received

This day the General Council of the Army met at Whitehall, where the draft of the "Agreement of the People" was subscribed by many officers present, and Sir Hardress Waller and sixteen other officers [were] nominated to present it next morning to the House of Commons.

A petition was this day presented to the General Council of the Army at Whitehall from the well-affected of the counties of North Wales. A petition well-penned, too large to be here inserted, but it is in full compliance with the "Remonstrance of the Army" and the petitions from several other counties to bring delinquents to punishment. And after the reading thereof, two officers of the Army were appointed to return the thanks of the Council to the gentlemen of North Wales who brought it, and also [to] signify unto them how much their hands were strengthened and their hearts encouraged to go on in the great affairs they are about by such a seasonable overture as this.

Excerpts from the "Agreement of the People"

In its petition, the General Council of the Army defends Pride's Purge and presses the House of Commons to endorse the Agreement and circulate it for signature around the country as the contractual foundation of a new national government

In our late Remonstrance of the eighteenth of November last we propounded (next after the matters of public justice) some foundations for a general settlement of peace in the nation which we therein desired might be formed and established in the nature of a General Contract or Agreement of the People. And, since then, the matters so propounded being wholly rejected, or no consideration of them admitted in Parliament (though visibly of highest moment to the public) and all ordinary remedies being denied, we were necessitated to an extraordinary way of remedy whereby to avoid the mischiefs then at hand and set you in a condition (without such obstructions or diversions by corrupt members) to proceed to matters of public justice and general settlement. Now as nothing did in our own hearts more justify our late undertakings towards many members in this Parliament than the necessity thereof in order to a sound settlement in the kingdom and the integrity of our intentions to make use of it only to that end, so we hold ourselves obliged to give the people all assurance possible that our opposing the corrupt closure [i.e., the Treaty of Newport] endeavored with the King was not in design to hinder peace or settlement (thereby to render our employments as soldiers necessary to be continued), and that neither that extraordinary course we have taken nor any other proceeding of ours have been intended for the setting up of any particular party or interest by or with which to uphold ourselves in power and dominion over the nation, but that it was and is the desire of our hearts in all we have done (with the hindering of that imminent evil and destructive conjunction with the King) to make way for a settlement of the peace and government of the kingdom upon grounds of common freedom and safety. And therefore, because our former overtures for that purpose (being only in general terms and not reduced to a certainty of particulars fit for practice) might possibly be understood but as plausible pretenses not intended really to be put into effect, we have thought it our duty to draw out those generals into an entire frame of particulars ascertained with such circumstances as may make it effectively practicable. And for that end, while your time hath been taken up in other matters of high and present importance, we have spent much of ours in preparing and perfecting such a draft of an Agreement, in all things so circumstantiated as to render it ripe for your speedier consideration and the kingdom's acceptance and practice, if approved. And so we do herewith humbly present it to you.

Now, to prevent misunderstanding of our intentions therein, we have but this to say: that we are far from such a spirit as positively to impose our private apprehensions upon the judgments of any in the kingdom that have not forfeited their freedom, and much less upon yourselves; neither are we apt in any wise to insist upon circumstantial things or aught that is not evidently fundamental to that public interest for which you and we have declared and engaged. But in this tender of it we humbly desire:

(1) That, whether it shall be fully approved by you and received by the people as it now stands or not, it may yet remain upon record before you, a perpetual witness of our real intentions and utmost endeavors for a sound and equal settlement, and as a testimony whereby all men may be assured what we are willing and ready to acquiesce in, and their jealousies satisfied or mouths stopped who are apt to think or say we have no bottom [i.e., no platform].

(2) That, with all expedition which the immediate and pressing great affairs will admit, it may receive your most mature consideration and resolutions upon it, not that we desire either the whole or what you shall like in it should be by your authority imposed as a law upon the kingdom (for so it would lose the intended nature of an Agreement of the People) but that, so far as it concurs with your own judgments, it may receive your seal of approbation only.

(3) That it may be tendered to the people in all parts to be subscribed by those that are willing, as petitions and other things of a voluntary nature are. And if, upon the account of subscriptions to be returned by those commissioners [entrusted with circulating the Agreement for signature] in April next, there appear to be a general or common reception of it amongst the people (or by the well-affected of them and such as are not obnoxious for delinquency) it may then take place and effect according to the tenor and substance of it.

Preamble to the Agreement

Having by our late labors and hazards made it appear to the world at how high a rate we value our just freedom, and God having so far owned our cause as to deliver the enemies thereof into our hands, we do now hold ourselves bound in mutual duty to each other to take the best care we can for the future to avoid both the danger of returning into a slavish condition and the chargeable [i.e., burdensome] remedy of another war. For as it cannot be imagined that so many of our countrymen would have opposed us in this quarrel if they had understood their own good, so may we hopefully promise to ourselves that when our common right and liberties shall be cleared, their endeavors will be disappointed that seek to make themselves our masters.

Since, therefore, our former oppressions and not-yet-ended troubles have been occasioned either by want of frequent National Meetings in Council, or by the undue or unequal constitution thereof, or by rendering those meetings ineffectual, we are fully agreed and resolved (God willing) to provide that hereafter our Representatives be neither left to an uncertainty for time, nor be unequally constituted, nor made useless to the ends for which they are intended. In order whereunto, *we declare and agree:*

Clause 1 of the Agreement—dissolution of the present Parliament

That to prevent the many inconveniences apparently arising from the long continuance of the same persons in supreme authority, this present Parliament end and dissolve upon or before the last day of April, in the year of our Lord 1649.

Clause 2—constituencies should be redistributed to provide more equitable representation in Parliament, henceforth referred to as the "Representative"

That the people of England (being at this day very unequally distributed by counties, cities, and boroughs for the election of their Representatives) be indifferently proportioned, and to this end that the Representative of the whole nation shall consist of four hundred persons or not above, and in each county and the places thereto subjoined there shall be chosen to make up the said Representative at all times the several numbers here mentioned [there follows a detailed list of constituencies].

Clause 3—biennial elections, a significantly extended franchise, and safeguards against corruption and conflict of interest are proposed

That the people do of course [i.e., routinely] choose themselves a Representative once in two years and shall meet for that purpose upon the first Thursday in every second May by 11 of the clock in the morning, and the Representatives so chosen to meet upon the second Thursday in June following at the usual place in Westminster (or such other place as by the foregoing Representative, or the Council of State in the interval, shall be from time to time appointed and published to the people at the least twenty days before the time of election) and to continue their session there (or elsewhere) until the second Thursday in December following, unless they shall adjourn or dissolve themselves sooner, but not to continue longer.

The election of the first Representative to be on the first Thursday in May, 1649. That and all future elections to be according to the rules prescribed for the same purpose in this Agreement, namely:

(1) That the electors in every division shall be natives or denizens of England, not persons receiving alms but such as are assessed [i.e., taxed] ordinarily towards the relief of the poor, not servants to and receiving wages from any particular person. And in all elections (except for the Universities), they shall be men of 21 years old or upwards and house-keepers dwelling within the division for which the election is provided. That until the end of seven years next ensuing the time herein limited for the end of this present Parliament, no person shall be admitted to or have any hand or voice in such elections who hath adhered unto or assisted the King against the Parliament in any [of] the late wars or insurrections, or who shall make or join in or abet any forcible opposition against this Agreement.

(4) That to the end all officers of state may be certainly accountable and no factions made to maintain corrupt interests, no member of a Council of State, nor any officer of any salary forces in [the] Army or garrison, nor any treasurer or receiver of public moneys shall (while such) be elected to be of a Representative. And in case any such election shall be, the same to be void. And in case any lawyer shall be chosen of any Representative or Council of State, then he shall be incapable of practice as a lawyer during that trust.

Clauses 5 and 6—executive power to be entrusted to a Council of State appointed by each Representative to govern the country for a two-year term

That each Representative shall within twenty days after their first meeting appoint a Council of State for the managing of public affairs until the tenth day after the meeting of the next Representative, unless that next Representative think fit to put an end to that trust sooner. And the same Council to act and proceed therein according to such instructions and limitations as the Representative shall give, and not otherwise.

That in each interval betwixt biennial Representatives, the Council of State (in case of imminent danger or extreme necessity) may summon a Representative to be forthwith chosen and to meet, so as the session thereof continue not above fourscore days and so as it dissolve at least fifty days before the appointed time for the next biennial Representative, and upon the fiftieth day so preceding it shall dissolve of course if not otherwise dissolved sooner.

Clause 8—how the powers of the Representative are to be defined and limited

That the Representatives have and shall be understood to have the supreme trust in order to the preservation and government of the whole, and that their power extend without the consent or concurrence of any other person or persons to the erecting and abolishing of courts of justice and public offices, and to the enacting, altering, repealing, and declaring of laws, and [to] the highest and final judgment concerning all natural or civil things, but not concerning things spiritual or evangelical, provided that even in things natural and civil these six particulars next following are and shall be understood to be excepted and reserved from our Representatives, namely:

(1) We do not empower them to impress or constrain any person to serve in foreign war either by sea or land, nor for any military service within the kingdom, save that they may take order for the forming, training, and exercising of the people in a military way to be in readiness for resisting of foreign invasions, suppressing of sudden insurrections, or for assisting in execution of law, and may take order for the employing and conducting of them for those ends, provided that even in such cases none be compellable to go out of the county he lives in if he procure another to serve in his room [i.e., place].

(2) That after the time herein limited for the commencement of the first Representative, none of the people may be at any time questioned for anything said or done in relation to the late wars or public differences, otherwise than in execution or pursuance of the determinations of the present House of Commons against such as have adhered to the King or his interest against the people, and saving that accountants [i.e., those accountable] for public moneys received shall remain accountable for the same.

(3) That no securities given, or to be given, by the public faith of the nation, nor any engagement of the public faith for satisfaction of debts and damages, shall be made void or invalid by the next or any future Representatives, except to such creditors as have, or shall have, justly forfeited the same, and saving that the next Representative may confirm or make null, in part or in whole, all gifts of lands, moneys, offices, or otherwise, made by the present Parliament to any member or attendant of either House.

(4) That in any laws hereafter to be made, no person by virtue of any tenure, grant, charter, patent, degree, or birth, shall be privileged from subjection thereto or from being bound thereby as well as others.

(5) That the Representative may not give judgment upon any man's person or estate where no law hath before provided, save only in calling to account and punishing public officers for abusing or failing their trust.

(6) That no Representative may in any wise render up, or give, or take away, any [of] the foundations of common right, liberty, and safety contained in this Agreement, nor level men's estates, destroy property, or make all things common.

Clause 9—a limited toleration of religious diversity is proposed

Concerning religion, we agree as followeth:

(1) It is intended that [the] Christian religion be held forth and recommended as the public profession in this nation, which we desire may (by the Grace of God) be reformed to the greatest purity in doctrine, worship, and discipline, according to the Word of God. The instructing of the people whereunto in a public way (so it be not compulsive), as also the maintaining of able teachers for that end and for the confutation or discovery of heresy, error, and whatsoever is contrary to sound doctrine, is allowed to be provided for by our Representatives,

the maintenance of which may be out of a public treasury and (we desire) not by tithes, provided that Popery or Prelacy be not held forth as the public way or profession in this nation.

(2) That to the public profession so held forth none be compelled by penalties or otherwise, but only may be endeavored to be won by sound doctrine and the example of a good conversation.

(3) That such as profess faith in God by Jesus Christ (however differing in judgment from the doctrine, worship, or discipline publicly held forth, as aforesaid) shall not be restrained from, but shall be protected in, the profession of their faith and exercise of religion according to their consciences in any place (except such as shall be set apart for the public worship, where we provide not for them unless they have leave), so as they abuse not this liberty to the civil injury of others or to actual disturbance of the public peace on their parts. Nevertheless, it is not intended to be hereby provided that this liberty shall necessarily extend to Popery or Prelacy.

Clause 10—treason and the right of rebellion

It is agreed that whosoever shall by force of arms resist the orders of the next or any future Representative (except in case where such Representative shall evidently render up, or give, or take away the foundations of common right, liberty, and safety contained in this Agreement) shall forthwith after his or their such resistance lose the benefit and protection of the laws and shall be punishable with death as an enemy and traitor to the nation.

Saturday, 20 January 1649

House of Commons

The Army presents the "Agreement of the People"

The House was informed that Lieutenant General Hammond and many other chief officers of the Army were at the door to present something of great concernment to them from the General Council of the Army. They ordered that they should be called in, which done by the Sergeant at Arms attending the House, they acquainted them that they were commanded by the General Council of the Army under His Excellency's command, and in the name of all the said Army, to present to their speedy and serious consideration a petition from the said General Council entitled "An Agreement of the People of England."

The chief officers withdrawing, the House ordered that the said petition should be read, which accordingly was done. And in respect they had ordered to rise at 12 o'clock in order to the King's trial, which was to hear his charge before the commissioners in Westminster Hall, they had not time then to hear the said Agreement. Whereupon they ordered that the thanks of the said House should be given to those gentlemen for their particular and great services to the whole kingdom, and that they should be desired to return their hearty thanks to the General Council of Officers and all the Army under the General's command for all their unwearied and gallant services to this nation, and that the said petition and their answer should be forthwith printed and published, that the kingdom may take notice of the union and affection between the Parliament and the Army. And the Agreement should be taken into speedy and serious consideration. The officers being again called in, Mr. Speaker returned them an answer to this purpose.

The House had debate upon report of a late conference between the King and Mr. Peters that the King very earnestly desired (for better satisfaction of some scruple of conscience) he might have one of his own chaplains admitted to him. The House hereupon ordered Dr. Juxon, late Lord Bishop of London, should be permitted to attend the King.

The House ordered that the Commissioners of the Great Seal should issue forth writs for adjournment of the next term, notwithstanding the Lords Commissioners' non-adherence.

Preliminary Proceedings of the High Court of Justice

Private meeting interrupted by a call from the House of Commons, as reported in Phelps's Journal

Three proclamations, and attendance commanded.

Ordered, that Sir Henry Mildmay be desired to deliver unto John Humphreys, Esq., the Sword of State in his custody, which said Sword the said Mr. Humphreys is to bear before the Lord President of this court.

The court being seated as aforesaid, before they engaged in further business the Sergeant at Arms of the House of Commons came thither and acquainted the court that the House wanted their members that were of that court. The court thereupon adjourned till 12 of the clock the same day.

The court reconvenes at noon in the Painted Chamber with fifty-seven commissioners present, as reported in Phelps's Journal

Here the court sat private.

Ordered, that the form and method of the court's proceeding unto and in the reading of the commission by which they sit, sending for and bringing in the Prisoner to the Bar, acquainting him in brief with the cause of his bringing thither, receiving and reading the charge, and demanding what the Prisoner says thereto, be referred to the discretion of the Lord President; as also that in case the Prisoner shall in language and carriage towards the court be insolent, outrageous, or contemptuous, that it be left to the Lord President to reprehend him therefore and admonish him of his duty, or to command the taking away of the Prisoner, and (if he see cause) to withdraw or adjourn the court. But as to the Prisoner's putting off his hat, the court will not insist upon it for this day. And that if the King desire time to answer, the Lord President is to give him time.

Ordered, upon the Lord President's desire and motion, that Mr. Lisle and Mr. Say, commissioners of this court, be assistants to the

Lord President. And for that purpose it is ordered that they sit near the Lord President in court.

Mr. Solicitor presented the charge against the King engrossed in parchment, which was read, and being by Mr. Solicitor signed, was returned to him to be exhibited against the King in his presence in open court. And thereupon the court adjourned itself forthwith to the Great Hall in Westminster.

The King's Trial Begins

The King is charged and refuses to plead—a contemporary published transcript of the first day of the trial in Westminster Hall, sixty-seven commissioners present

On Saturday, being the twentieth day of January, 1649, the Lord President of the High Court of Justice with near four score of the members of the said court, having sixteen gentlemen with partizans and a Sword and a Mace with their and other officers of the said court marching before them, came to the place ordered to be prepared for their sitting at the west end of the Great Hall at Westminster, where the Lord President in a crimson velvet chair fixed in the midst of the court placed himself, having a desk with a crimson velvet cushion before him, the rest of the members placing themselves on each side of him upon the several seats or benches prepared and hung with

The High Court in Session: Westminster Hall is crammed with spectators, soldiers, and court officers. The King sits alone, facing Lord President Bradshaw and the other commissioners. Set between the King and his judges is the Clerks' table, on which lie the Mace and Sword of State along with a copy of the charge. Standing to the King's right are John Cook, the prosecutor, and his two assistants. In keeping with the then-normal practice at treason trials, there is no defense counsel. Westminster Hall's size and rich associations made it an ideal setting for the proceedings. The Courts of King's Bench and Chancery had their normal home under the window where Charles's judges now sit; the Court of Common Pleas usually occupied the other end of the hall. In fact, the King's trial necessitated dismantling the partitions surrounding these courts and postponing for two weeks the start of their next session. The greatest of the state trials, as well as the depositions of Edward II and Richard II, had been held in Westminster Hall over its five-and-a-half century history. As one of the commissioners later recalled, Charles's trial "was not a thing done in a corner." Indeed, if a single building represented the timeless majesty of English law, it was Westminster Hall. Engraving from John Nalson, *A True Copy of the Journal of the High Court of Justice for the Tryal of K. Charles I* (London, 1684). By courtesy of the Huntington Library, San Marino, California.

scarlet for that purpose, and the partizans dividing themselves on each side of the court before them.

The court being thus seated and silence made, the great gate of the said hall was set open to the end that all persons (without exception) desirous to see or hear might come into it, upon which the hall was presently filled and silence again ordered.

This done, Colonel Thomlinson, who had the charge of the Prisoner, was commanded to bring him to the court, who within a quarter of an hour's space brought him, attended with about twenty officers with partizans marching before him, there being other gentlemen to whose care and custody he was likewise committed marching in his rear.

Being thus brought up within the face of the court, the Sergeant at Arms with his Mace receives and conducts him straight to the Bar, having a crimson velvet chair set before him. After a stern looking upon the court and the people in the galleries on each side of him, he places himself, not at all moving his hat or otherwise showing the least respect to the court, but presently rises up again and turns about, looking downwards upon the guards placed on the left side and on the multitude of spectators on the right side of the said Great Hall.

After silence made among the people, the act of Parliament for the trying of Charles Stuart, King of England, was read over by the Clerk of the Court, who sat on one side of a table covered with a rich Turkey carpet and placed at the feet of the said Lord President, upon which table was also laid the Sword and Mace. After reading the said act, the several names of the commissioners were called over, every one who was present rising up and answering his call.

[The Prisoner] having again placed himself in his chair with his face towards the court, silence being again ordered, the Lord President stood up and said: "Charles Stuart, King of England, the Commons of England assembled in Parliament, being deeply sensible of the calamities that have been brought upon this nation (which is fixed upon you as the principal author of it) have resolved to make inquisition for blood, and according to that debt and duty they owe to justice, to God, the kingdom, and themselves, and according to the fundamental power that rests in themselves, they have resolved to bring you to trial and judgment, and for that purpose have constituted this High Court of Justice before which you are brought."

This said, Mr. Cook, Attorney for the Commonwealth, standing within the Bar on the right hand of the Prisoner, offered to speak, but the King, having a staff in his hand, held it up and laid it upon the said Mr. Cook's shoulder two or three times, bidding him hold. Nevertheless, the Lord President ordering him to go on, Mr. Cook said: "My lord, I am commanded to charge Charles Stuart, King of England, in the name of the Commons of England, with treason and high misdemeanors. I desire the said charge may be read."

The said charge being delivered to the Clerk of the Court, the Lord President ordered it should be read, but the King bid him hold. Nevertheless, being commanded by the Lord President to read it, the Clerk began:

The Charge of the Commons of England against Charles Stuart, King of England, of High Treason and other high crimes, exhibited to the High Court of Justice.

That [he] the said Charles Stuart, being admitted King of England and therein trusted with a limited power to govern by and according to the laws of the land and not otherwise, and by his trust, oath, and office being obliged to use the power committed to him for the good and benefit of the people and for the preservation of their rights and liberties, yet nevertheless out of a wicked design to erect and uphold in himself an unlimited and tyrannical power to rule according to his will, and to overthrow the rights and liberties of the people, yea to take away and make void the foundations thereof and of all redress and remedy of misgovernment, which by the fundamental constitutions of this kingdom were reserved on the people's behalf in the right and power of frequent and successive Parliaments or National Meetings in Council, he (the said Charles Stuart) for accomplishment of such his designs and for the protecting of himself and his adherents in his and their wicked practices to the same ends, hath traitorously and maliciously levied war against the present Parliament and the people therein represented, particularly upon or about the thirtieth day of June in the year of our Lord 1642 at Beverley in the county of York; and upon or about the thirtieth day of July in the year aforesaid in the county of the city of York; and upon or about the twenty-fourth day of August in the same year at the county of the

town of Nottingham, when and where he set up his standard
of war; and also on or about the twenty-third day of October
in the same year at Edgehill and Kineton Field in the county of
Warwick; and upon or about the thirtieth day of November in
the same year at Brentford in the county of Middlesex; and
upon or about the thirtieth day of August in the year of our
Lord 1643 at Caversham Bridge, near Reading, in the county
of Berks; and upon or about the thirtieth day of October in the year
last mentioned at or near the city of Gloucester; and upon or
about the thirtieth day of November in the year last mentioned at Newbury in the county of Berks; and upon or about
the thirty-first day of July in the year of our Lord 1644 at
Cropredy Bridge in the county of Oxon; and upon or about
the thirtieth day of September in the last year mentioned at
Bodmin and other places near adjacent in the county of
Cornwall; and upon or about the thirtieth day of November in
the year last mentioned at Newbury aforesaid; and upon or
about the eighth day of June in the year of our Lord 1645 at
the town of Leicester; and also upon the fourteenth day of the
same month in the same year at Naseby Field in the county of
Northampton. At which several times and places (or most of
them) and at many other places in this land, at several other
times within the years aforementioned and in the year of our
Lord 1646, he (the said Charles Stuart) hath caused and procured many thousands of the free people of this nation to be
slain, and by divisions, parties and insurrections within this
land, by invasions from foreign parts endeavored and procured by him, and by many other evil ways and means, he
(the said Charles Stuart) hath not only maintained and carried
on the said war both by land and sea during the years before-
mentioned, but also hath renewed or caused to be renewed
the said war against the Parliament and good people of this
nation in this present year 1648/49 in the counties of Kent,
Essex, Surrey, Sussex, Middlesex, and many other counties
and places in England and Wales, and also by sea. And particularly he (the said Charles Stuart) hath for that purpose given
commission to his son the Prince and others whereby (besides
multitudes of other persons) many such as were by the
Parliament entrusted and employed for the safety of the

nation, being by him or his agents corrupted to the betraying of their trust and revolting from the Parliament, have had entertainment and commission for the continuing and renewing of war and hostility against the said Parliament and people as aforesaid. By which cruel and unnatural wars by him (the said Charles Stuart) levied, continued and renewed as aforesaid, much innocent blood of the free people of this nation hath been spilt, many families have been undone, the public treasury wasted and exhausted, trade obstructed and miserably decayed, vast expense and damage to the nation incurred, and many parts of the land spoiled, some of them even to desolation. And for further prosecution of his said evil designs, he (the said Charles Stuart) doth still continue his commissions to the said Prince and other rebels and revolters, both English and foreigners, and to the Earl of Ormonde and to the Irish rebels and revolters associated with him, from whom further invasions upon this land are threatened upon the procurement and on the behalf of the said Charles Stuart.

All which wicked designs, wars, and evil practices of him (the said Charles Stuart) have been and are carried on for the advancing and upholding of the personal interest of will and power and pretended prerogative to himself and his family against the public interest, common right, liberty, justice, and peace of the people of this nation, by and for whom he was entrusted as aforesaid.

By all which it appeareth that he (the said Charles Stuart) hath been and is the occasioner, author and continuer of the said unnatural, cruel, and bloody wars, and therein guilty of all the treasons, murders, rapines, burnings, spoils, desolations, damage, and mischief to this nation, acted or committed in the said wars or occasioned thereby.

And the said John Cook, by protestation (saving on the behalf of the people of England the liberty of exhibiting at any time hereafter any other charge against the said Charles Stuart, and also of replying to the answers which the said Charles Stuart shall make to the premises, or any of them, or any other charge that shall be so exhibited) doth for the said treasons and crimes on the behalf of the said people of England impeach the said Charles Stuart as a tyrant, traitor,

murderer, and a public and implacable enemy to the
Commonwealth of England and [doth] pray that the said
Charles Stuart, King of England, may be put to answer all
and every the premises, that such proceedings, examinations,
trials, sentence, and judgment may be thereupon had as shall
be agreeable to justice.

It is observed that the time the charge was reading, the King sat
down in his chair, looking sometimes on the court, sometimes up to
the galleries, and having risen again and turned about to behold the
guards and spectators, [he] sat down looking very sternly and with a
countenance not at all moved, till these words, "Charles Stuart,
tyrant, traitor, etc." were read, at which he laughed as he sat in the
face of the court.

The charge being read, the Lord President replied: "Sir, you have
now heard your charge read, containing such matter as appears in it.
You find that in the close of it, it is prayed to the court in the behalf of
the Commons of England that you answer to your charge. The court
expects your answer."

The King: I would know by what power I am called hither. I was
not long ago in the Isle of Wight. How I came there is a longer
story than I think is fit at this time for me to speak of. But there I
entered into a treaty with both Houses of Parliament with as
much public faith as it's possible to be had of any people in the
world. I treated there with a number of honorable lords and
gentlemen, and treated honestly and uprightly; I cannot say but
they did very nobly with me. We were upon a conclusion of the
treaty. Now, I would know by what authority—I mean lawful—there are many unlawful authorities in the world—thieves
and robbers by the highways—but I would know by what
authority I was brought from thence and carried from place to
place, and I know not what. And when I know what lawful
authority, I shall answer. Remember, I am your King—your
lawful King—and what sins you bring upon your heads and the
judgment of God upon this land, think well upon it—I say think
well upon it—before you go further from one sin to a greater.
Therefore let me know by what lawful authority I am seated
here and I shall not be unwilling to answer. In the meantime, I

shall not betray my trust. I have a trust committed to me by God, by old and lawful descent [i.e., by hereditary right]. I will not betray it to answer to a new unlawful authority. Therefore, resolve me that, and you shall hear more of me.

Lord President: If you had been pleased to have observed what was hinted to you by the court at your first coming hither, you would have known by what authority. Which authority requires you—in the name of the people of England, of which you are elected King—to answer them.

The King: No, sir, I deny that.

Lord President: If you acknowledge not the authority of the court, they must proceed.

The King: I do tell them so—England was never an elective kingdom but an hereditary kingdom for near these thousand years. Therefore, let me know by what authority I am called hither. I do stand more for the liberty of my people than any here that come to be my pretended judges. And therefore let me know by what lawful authority I am seated here, and I will answer it. Otherwise I will not answer it.

Lord President: Sir, how really you have managed your trust is known. Your way of answer is to interrogate the court, which beseems not you in this condition. You have been told of it twice or thrice.

The King: Here is a gentleman, Lieutenant Colonel Cobbet—ask him if he did not bring me from the Isle of Wight by force. I do not come here as submitting to the court. I will stand as much for the privilege of the House of Commons, rightly understood, as any man here whatsoever. I see no House of Lords here that may constitute a Parliament, and the King too should have been. Is this the bringing of the King to his Parliament? Is this the bringing an end to the treaty in the public faith of the world? Let me see a legal authority warranted by the Word of God—the Scriptures—or warranted by the constitutions of the kingdom, and I will answer.

Lord President: Sir, you have propounded a question and have been answered. Seeing you will not answer, the court will consider how to proceed. In the meantime, those that brought you hither are to take charge of you back again. The court desires to know whether this be all the answer you will give or no.

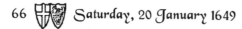

The King: Sir, I desire that you would give me and all the world satisfaction in this. Let me tell you, it is not a slight thing you are about. I am sworn to keep the peace by that duty I owe to God and my country, and I will do it to the last breath of my body. And therefore you shall do well to satisfy first God, and then the country, by what authority you do it. If you do it by a usurped authority, that will not last long. There is a God in Heaven that will call you and all that give you power to account. Satisfy me in that, and I will answer; otherwise I betray my trust and the liberties of the people. And therefore think of that, and then I shall be willing. For I do avow that it is as great a sin to withstand [i.e., resist] lawful authority as it is to submit to a tyrannical or any otherwise unlawful authority. And therefore satisfy God and me and all the world in that, and you shall receive my answer. I am not afraid of the Bill [i.e., the Bill of Attainder lying on the Clerks' table].

Lord President: The court expects you should give them a final answer. Their purpose is to adjourn till Monday next if you do not satisfy yourself, though we do tell you our authority. We are satisfied with our authority, and it is upon God's authority and the kingdom's. And that peace you speak of will be kept in the doing of justice, and that's our present work.

The King: Let me tell you, if you will show me what lawful authority you have, I shall be satisfied. But that you have said satisfies no reasonable man.

Lord President: That's in your apprehension. We think it reasonable that are your judges.

The King: 'Tis not my apprehension—nor yours either—that ought to decide it.

Lord President: The court hath heard you, and you are to be disposed of as they have commanded.

Two things were remarkable in this day's proceedings: (1) it is to be observed that as the charge was reading against the King, the silver head of his staff fell off, the which he wondered at, and seeing none to take it up, he stoops for it himself; (2) that as the King was going away, he looked with a very austere countenance upon the court, with stirring of his hat replied "Well, sir" when the Lord President commanded the guard to take him away, and at his going

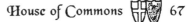

down he said "I do not fear that" (pointing with his staff at the Sword). The people in the hall as he went down the stairs cried out, some "God save the King!" and some for "Justice!"

Oyez being called, the court adjourned till Monday next, January 22, at nine in the morning to the Painted Chamber, and from thence to the same place again in Westminster Hall.

Other News

Lady Fairfax speaks out at the trial against her husband's inclusion among the King's judges

It is to be remembered that at this time the Lady Fairfax (wife to the General), being above in a window, interrupted the reading of the names of the commissioners by speaking aloud to the court then sitting that her husband, the Lord Fairfax, was not there in person, nor ever would sit among them, and therefore they did him wrong to name him as a sitting commissioner.

People flock to see the King

On Saturday great concourse of people went out of London to Westminster, but if to see the King they were disappointed, who was then at St. James's under a strong guard. A solemn Fast was kept at Whitehall this day by the commissioners for trial of the King.

Monday, 22 January 1649

House of Commons

Scottish protests against the King's trial

This day the commissioners for the Kingdom of Scotland delivered into the House of Commons some papers and a declaration from the Parliament of Scotland, wherein they express a dislike of the present proceedings about the trial of the King and declare: that the Kingdom of Scotland has an undoubted interest in the person of the

A Description of the High Court of Justice : 1648

A y.e Lord president
B y.e King

C Councell
D Clarkes

E Guard
F Galleries

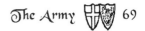

King, who was not (they say) delivered to the English commissioners at Newcastle for the ruin of his person but for a more speedy settlement of the peace of his kingdoms; that they extremely dissent and declare against the trial of him; and that this present way of proceeding against him leaves a deep impression on them and sits heavy on all their spirits in regard of the great miseries that are like to ensue upon these kingdoms. The Scots commissioners by their papers further moved the House that they might have leave to make their personal addresses to the King.

The House, upon reading the whole, referred it to committee to draw up an answer to the Parliament of Scotland. This declaration with some other papers from the Parliament of Scotland were likewise pretended [i.e., submitted] by the Scots commissioners to His Excellency the Lord Fairfax.

The Army

Support for the purge of Parliament and the King's trial—a letter to Lord Fairfax from the forces besieging Pontefract

May it please Your Excellency,

By understanding that the Commons of England in Parliament have lately voted the supreme power of the kingdom to be in the people and derivatively in them (their representatives) for the making, repealing and confirming all laws, and by virtue of that power have appointed an High Court of Justice for the trial of the King, as also to bring to justice other captivated enemies of our peace and freedoms, we begin to see some hopes of reaping the happy fruits of our hard labors and long services for the settling of this

Another View of the Trial: This contemporary engraving gives a better sense of the crush of spectators filling Westminster Hall, some in galleries and others at floor level. The strategic placement of troops and barriers reveals the court's fear that the trial might be disrupted. Indeed, despite frequent warnings from the bench, there were cheers and spontaneous expressions of support for Charles. It was from one of the window seats at the side that Lady Fairfax made her memorable interruption, declaring that her husband would never sit in judgment of the King. In fact, Lord Fairfax was not alone: of the one hundred thirty-five commissioners named to the High Court, only fifty-nine signed the death warrant and forty-seven never attended a single session. By courtesy of the Department of Western Art, Ashmolean Museum, Oxford.

nation in the enjoyment thereof and are unable sufficiently to express our joyful resentment [i.e., appreciation] of your late most necessary wisely-managed action in securing and secluding those members of the House that carried on that series of wicked, corrupt, and treacherous counsel and design to betray the kingdom to perpetual slavery for their own ends, largely mentioned in your remonstrances, declarations, and more particularly in your late humble answer to the Parliament's demand of the reason of your securing and secluding the said members, which we hope has given them (as we doubt not all well-affected unprejudiced people thereby will with us receive) full satisfaction thereunto, and that they will plainly perceive the good hand of God leading you to and acting you in that high and harmless service of the kingdom as a manifest token of His Presence, and that very way He had appointed to break in pieces those strange destructive counsels which doubtless would have soon involved the kingdom in more war and troubles, to its utter ruin.

Neither can we hide our great rejoicing to see your prudence, care, and constancy in the kingdom's present necessary work, nor our observation of that presence, power, and wisdom of God carrying you on therein, which as we doubt not but the Parliament and all the well affected at least will see, and the whole kingdom (though most unworthy) enjoy the benefit of, so you also (upon your humble, careful, and tender walking in your high and slippery places) will conceive a continuation of this Divine Presence, not only to the silencing and preventing of all your enemies who watch and labor for your falling, but even in the perfecting of the same, so as all the people shall acknowledge it is the Work of God alone.

Signed in the name of the Council of Officers at the leaguer before Pontefract Castle,

Thomas Margetts

Pontefract
January 19, 1649

Preliminary Proceedings of the High Court of Justice

Private meeting in the Painted Chamber, sixty-two commissioners present,
as reported in Phelps's Journal

Here the court sit private.

Colonel Harvey informeth the court that he was desired to signify unto this court in the behalf of Mr. John Corbet, member of this court, that his absence is not from any disaffection to the proceedings of this court but in regard of other especial employment that he hath in the service of the state.

Here the court considered of the King's carriage on the Saturday before and of all that had then passed on the court's behalf, and approved thereof as agreeing to their sense and directions. And perceiving what the King aimed at—namely to bring in question, if he could, the jurisdiction of the court and the authority whereby they sat—and considering that he had not in the interim acknowledged them in any sort to be a court or in any judicial capacity to determine of his demand and plea, and that through their sides he intended to wound—if he might be permitted—the supreme authority of the Commons of England in their representative, the Commons assembled in Parliament, after advice with their counsel learned in both laws, and mature deliberation had of the matter: Resolved, that the Prisoner should not be suffered to bring these things in question which he aimed at, touching that highest jurisdiction, whereof they might not make themselves judges and from which there was no appeal.

And [the court] therefore order and direct: Ordered, that in case the King shall again offer to fall into that discourse the Lord President do let him know that the court have taken into consideration his demands of the last day and that he ought to rest satisfied with this answer, that the Commons of England assembled in Parliament have constituted this court, whose power may not nor should not be permitted to be disputed by him, and that they were resolved he should answer his charge. That in case he shall refuse to answer or acknowledge the court, the Lord President do let him know that the court will take it as a contumacy and that it shall be so recorded. That in case he shall offer to answer with a saving, notwithstanding, of his pretended prerogative, that the Lord President do in the name of the court

refuse his protest and require his positive answer to the charge. That in case the King shall demand a copy of the charge, that he shall then declare his intention to answer, and that declaring such his intention a copy be granted unto him. That in case the King shall still persist in his contempt, the Lord President do give command to the Clerk to demand of the King in the name of the court, in these words following:

> Charles Stuart, King of England, you are accused in the behalf
> of the people of England of divers high crimes and treasons,
> which charge hath been read unto you. The court requires
> you to give a positive answer whether you confess or deny
> the charge, having determined that you ought to answer the
> same.

Ordered, that the commissioners shall be called in open court at the court's sitting in the hall, and that the names of such as appear shall be recorded.

Hereupon the court forthwith adjourned itself into Westminster Hall.

Charles I at His Trial: From a vantage point in one of the forward galleries, a painter named Edward Bower witnessed the trial and made sketches for what was to be Charles's last portrait. Its details are eloquent. Dressed in black, Charles sits in a crimson velvet chair, facing his judges with tense dignity. His graying beard is uncharacteristically full, due to the fact that he was refusing the services of a barber. Around his neck is the Lesser George, the insignia of the Order of the Garter that he would wear to the scaffold. His left hand holds the staff mentioned in the records of the first day of the trial when—unexpectedly and ominously—its silver head fell off after Charles attempted to use it to interrupt the Solicitor's presentation of the charge. The folded paper in his right hand could contain notes for the speech of protest he was not allowed to give. Although Charles's judges could stifle his words, they hesitated to challenge his tall black hat. To wear it defiantly in their presence was a proof of his regality and symbolic of his rejection of their authority, as was his refusal to enter a plea. That Charles's judges decided to ignore the hat would prompt a royalist to quip that "they, who thought it not manners to take off his hat, yet thought it no sin to take off his Sacred Head." This portrait has long been in the possession of the Carew family, whose own vicissitudes illustrate the deep divisions of the Civil War. Sir Alexander Carew was executed for treason against the parliamentary cause in 1644; his brother John was one of the King's judges. John faithfully attended the trial, signed the death warrant, and upon the Restoration was himself condemned to a traitor's death. Antony House, Cornwall. Reproduced by kind permission of Sir John Carew Pole, Bart. Photo by courtesy of the Royal Academy of Arts.

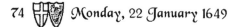

The King's Trial Continues

*The King persists in refusing to recognize the court—a contemporary
published transcript of the second day of the trial in Westminster Hall,
seventy commissioners present*

Oyez made. Silence commanded. The court called and answered
to their names. Silence commanded upon pain of imprisonment, and
the Captain of the Guard to apprehend all such as make disturbance.

Upon the King's coming in, a shout was made. Command given
by the court to the Captain of the Guard to fetch and take into his custody those who make any disturbance.

Mr. Solicitor: May it please your lordship, my Lord President. I
did at the last court in the behalf of the Commons of England
exhibit and give into this court a charge of High Treason and
other high crimes against the Prisoner at the Bar, whereof I do
accuse him in the name of the people of England, and the charge
was read unto him and his answer required. My lord, he was
not then pleased to give an answer, but instead of answering did
there dispute the authority of this High Court. My humble
motion to this High Court, in behalf of the Kingdom of England,
is that the Prisoner may be directed to make a positive answer
either by way of confession or negation, which if he shall refuse
to do, that the matter of charge be taken as confessed and the
court may proceed according to justice.

Lord President: Sir, you may remember, at the last court you
were told the occasion of your being brought hither and you
heard a charge against you containing a charge of High Treason
and other high crimes against this realm of England. You heard
likewise that it was prayed in the behalf of the people that you
should give an answer to that charge, that thereupon such proceedings might be had as should be agreeable to justice. You
were then pleased to make some scruples concerning the
authority of this court, and knew not by what authority you
were brought hither. You did divers times propound your questions and were as often answered that it was by authority of the
Commons of England assembled in Parliament that did think fit
to call you to account for those high and capital misdemeanors

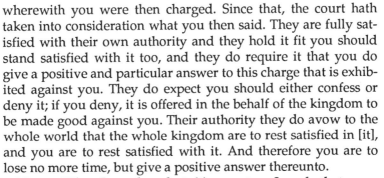

wherewith you were then charged. Since that, the court hath taken into consideration what you then said. They are fully satisfied with their own authority and they hold it fit you should stand satisfied with it too, and they do require it that you do give a positive and particular answer to this charge that is exhibited against you. They do expect you should either confess or deny it; if you deny, it is offered in the behalf of the kingdom to be made good against you. Their authority they do avow to the whole world that the whole kingdom are to rest satisfied in [it], and you are to rest satisfied with it. And therefore you are to lose no more time, but give a positive answer thereunto.

The King: When I was here last, 'tis very true I made that question. And truly, if it were only my own particular case, I would have satisfied myself with the protestation I made the last time I was here against the legality of this court and that a King cannot be tried by any superior jurisdiction on earth. But it is not my case alone—it is the freedom and the liberty of the people of England. And do you pretend what you will, I stand more for their liberties—for if power without law may make laws, may alter the fundamental laws of the kingdom, I do not know what subject he is in England that can be sure of his life or anything that he calls his own. Therefore, when that I came here I did expect particular reasons to know by what law, what authority, you did proceed against me here. And therefore I am a little to seek [i.e., a little puzzled about] what to say to you in this particular because the affirmative is to be proved, the negative often is very hard to do. But since I cannot persuade you to do it, I shall tell you my reasons as short as I can. My reasons why—in conscience and the duty I owe to God first, and my people next, for the preservation of their lives, liberties, and estates—I conceive I cannot answer this till I be satisfied of the legality of it. All proceedings against any man whatsoever—

Lord President: Sir, I must interrupt you, which I would not do, but that what you do is not agreeable to the proceedings of any court of justice. You are about to enter into argument and dispute concerning the authority of this court, before whom you appear as a prisoner and are charged as an high delinquent. If you take upon you to dispute the authority of the court, we may not do it, nor will any court give way unto it. You are to submit unto it. You are to give in a punctual and direct answer whether you will answer your charge or no, and what your answer is.

The King: Sir, by your favor, I do not know the forms of law; I do know law and reason, though. I am no lawyer professed, but I know as much law as any gentleman in England, and therefore (under favor) I do plead for the liberties of the people of England more than you do. And therefore, if I should impose a belief upon any man without reasons given for it, it were unreasonable. But I must tell you that that reason that I have, as thus informed, I cannot yield unto it—

Lord President: Sir, I must interrupt you. You may not be permitted. You speak of law and reason. It is fit there should be law and reason, and there is both against you. Sir, the vote of the Commons of England assembled in Parliament—it is the reason of the kingdom. And they [i.e., the Commons] are these that have given [being] to that law according to which you should have ruled and reigned. Sir, you are not to dispute our authority—you are told it again by the court. Sir, it will be taken notice of that you stand in contempt of the court, and your contempt will be recorded accordingly.

The King: I do not know how a King may be a delinquent. But by any law that ever I heard of, all men—delinquents, or what you will—let me tell you, they may put in demurrers against any proceeding as legal. And I do demand that, and demand to be heard with my reasons. If you deny that, you deny reason.

Lord President: Sir, you have offered something to the court. I shall speak something unto you—the sense of the court. Sir, neither you nor any man are permitted to dispute that point. You are concluded. You may not demur [to] the jurisdiction of the court—if you do, I must let you know that they overrule your demurrer. They sit here by the authority of the Commons of England, and all your predecessors and you are responsible to them—

The King: I deny that. Show me one precedent.

Lord President: Sir, you ought not to interrupt while the court is speaking to you. This point is not to be debated by you, neither will the court permit you to do it. If you offer it by way of demurrer to the jurisdiction of the court, they have considered of their jurisdiction. They do affirm their own jurisdiction.

The King: I say, sir, by your favor, that the Commons of England was never a court of judicature. I would know how they came to be so.

Lord President: Sir, you are not to be permitted to go on in that speech and these discourses.

Then the Clerk of the Court read as followeth: "Charles Stuart, King of England, you have been accused on the behalf of the people of England of High Treason and other high crimes. The court have determined that you ought to answer the same."

The King: I will answer the same so soon as I know by what authority you do this.

Lord President: If this be all that you will say, then, gentlemen—you that brought the Prisoner hither—take charge of him back again.

The King: I do require that I may give in my reasons why I do not answer. And give me time for that.

Lord President: Sir, 'tis not for prisoners to require.

The King: Prisoners? Sir, I am not an ordinary prisoner!

Lord President: The court hath considered of their jurisdiction, and they have already affirmed their jurisdiction. If you will not answer, we shall give order to record your default.

The King: You never heard my reasons yet.

Lord President: Sir, your reasons are not to be heard against the highest jurisdiction.

The King: Show me that jurisdiction where reason is not to be heard.

Lord President: Sir, we show it you here, the Commons of England. And the next time you are brought you will know more of the pleasure of the court, and (it may be) their final determination.

The King: Show me where ever the House of Commons was a court of judicature of that kind.

Lord President: Sergeant—take away the Prisoner.

The King: Well, sir, remember that the King is not suffered to give in his reasons for the liberty and freedom of all his subjects.

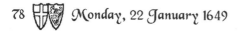

Lord President: Sir, you are not to have liberty to use this language. How great a friend you have been to the laws and liberties of the people, let all England and the world judge.

The King: Sir, under favor, it was the liberty, freedom, and laws of the subject that ever I took—defended myself with arms. I never took up arms against the people, but for the laws.

Lord President: The command of the court must be obeyed. No answer will be given to the charge.

The King: Well, sir.

Then the Lord President ordered the default to be recorded and the contempt of the court and that no answer would be given to the charge. And so he was guarded forth to Sir Robert Cotton's house.

Then the court adjourned to the Painted Chamber on Tuesday at 12 o'clock, and from thence they intend to adjourn to Westminster Hall, at which time all persons concerned are to give their attendance.

The King's Objections to the Court's Jurisdiction

The court's proceedings are illegal, contrary to the popular will, and an affront to the true privileges of Parliament—text of the speech the King was not permitted to give at his trial, with his own annotations

Having already made my protestations, not only against the illegality of this pretended court, but also that no earthly power can justly call me (who am your King) in question as a delinquent, I would not any more open my mouth upon this occasion more than to refer

The Divine Monarch in his True Parliament: This engraving first appeared ca. 1630 and shows Charles enthroned in the House of Lords. He sits in majesty, showered by Grace, and flanked by his Lords Spiritual and Temporal, clearly men who were prepared to pray and fight on his behalf. At the bottom stand his loyal Commons, hearts aflame with love and purses open, ready to pay the needful expenses of England's Continental allies Holland, Denmark, the Palatinate, and La Rochelle, grateful personifications of which appear beneath the throne. Charles argued in his ungiven speech of 22 January that he had a "duty . . . to God in the preservation of the true liberty of my people," and this picture conveys something of what he had in mind. As his father had put it, "the true law of free monarchies" required a king whose acts and desires remained wholly unconstrained by the wishes of his subjects. Anonymous engraving. By courtesy of the Department of Prints and Drawings, British Museum.

myself to what I have spoken were I in this case alone concerned. But the duty I owe to God in the preservation of the true liberty of my people will not suffer me at this time to be silent. For how can any freeborn subject of England call life or anything he possesseth his own, if power without right daily make new and abrogate the old fundamental law of the land, which I now take to be the present case. Wherefore, when I came hither I expected that you would have endeavored to have satisfied me concerning these grounds which hinder me to answer to your pretended impeachment. But since I see that nothing I can say will move you to it (though negatives are not so naturally proved as affirmatives) yet I will show you the reason why I am confident you cannot judge me, nor indeed the meanest man in England. For I will not (like you) without showing a reason seek to impose a belief upon my subjects.

There is no proceeding [that is] just against any man but what is warranted either by God's laws or the municipal laws of the country where he lives. (*Hereabout I was stopped and not suffered to speak any more concerning reasons.*) Now, I am most confident this day's proceeding cannot be warranted by God's law, for on the contrary the authority of obedience unto kings is clearly warranted and strictly commanded both in the Old and New Testament, which if denied I am ready instantly to prove. And for the question now in hand, there it is said that "Where the word of a king is, there is power: and who may say unto him, What doest thou?" [Eccles. 8:4]. Then for the law of this land, I am no less confident that no learned lawyer will affirm that an impeachment can lie against the King, they all going in his name. And one of their maxims is that the King can do no wrong. Besides, the law upon which you ground your proceedings must either be old or new. If old, show it; if new, tell what authority warranted by the fundamental laws of the land hath made it, and when. But how the House of Commons can erect a court of judicature, which was never one itself (as is well known to all lawyers) I leave to God and the world to judge. And it were full as strange that they should pretend to make laws without King or Lords' House, to any that have heard speak of the laws of England.

And admitting (but not granting) that the people of England's commission could grant your pretended power, I see nothing you can show for that, for certainly you never asked the question of the tenth man in the kingdom. And in this way you manifestly wrong even the poorest plowman if you demand not his free consent. Nor can you pretend any color for this your pretended commission without the consent at least of the major part of every man in England of whatsoever quality or condition, which I am sure you never went about to seek, so far are you from having it. Thus you see that I speak not for my own right alone, as I am your King, but also for the true liberty of all my subjects, which consists not in the power of government, but in living under such laws, such a government, as may give themselves the best assurance of their lives and property of their goods.

Nor in this must or do I forget the privileges of both Houses of Parliament which this day's proceedings do not only violate, but likewise occasion the greatest breach of their public faith that (I believe) ever was heard of, with which I am far from charging the two Houses, for all pretended crimes laid against me bear date long before this treaty at Newport, in which I having concluded as much as in me lay and hopefully expecting the Houses' agreement thereunto, I was suddenly surprised and hurried from thence as a prisoner, upon which account I am against my will brought hither, where (since I am come) I cannot but to my power defend the ancient laws and liberties of this kingdom together with my own just right. Then, for anything I can see, the Higher House is totally excluded. And, for the House of Commons, it is too well known that the major part of them are detained or deterred from sitting. So as if I had no other, this were sufficient for me to protest against the lawfulness of your pretended court.

Besides all this, the peace of the kingdom is not the least in my thoughts. And what hope of settlement is there, so long as power reigns without rule or law, changing the whole frame of that government under which this kingdom hath flourished for many hundred years? Nor will I say what will fall out in case this lawless, unjust proceeding against me do go on. And believe it, the Commons of England will not thank you for this change, for they will remember how happy they have been of late years under the reigns of Queen Elizabeth, the King my father, and myself, until the beginning of these unhappy troubles, and will have cause to doubt that they shall ever be so happy under any new. And by this time it will be too sensibly evident that the arms I took up were only to defend the fundamental laws of this kingdom against those who have supposed my power hath totally changed the ancient government.

Thus having showed you briefly the reasons why I cannot submit to your pretended authority without violating the trust which I have from God for the welfare and liberty of my people, I expect from you either clear reasons to convince my judgment, showing me that I am in an error (and then truly I will answer), or that you will withdraw your proceedings.

This I intended to speak in Westminster Hall on Monday, January 22, but against reason was hindered to show my reasons.

Tuesday, 23 January 1649

House of Commons

Ordinance for altering judicial procedures reported

The Commons this day had an ordinance reported for settling of the courts of justice and in what way writs should be issued for the future: that writs out of Chancery should go in the name of Chancellor or Keepers of the Seal, also in other courts in the name of the judge or judges. And whereas it has been formerly charged upon malefactors that they have acted "contrary to the Peace of our Sovereign Lord the King, his Crown and Dignity," it is now to be thus, "against the Peace, Justice, and Council of England."

Preliminary Proceedings of the High Court of Justice

The court grapples with the King's refusal to enter a plea—private meeting in the Painted Chamber, sixty-three commissioners present, as reported in Phelps's Journal

Here the court sat private.

And taking into consideration the proceeding of the last court the last day, [the court] fully approved of what in their behalf had been then said and done. And likewise, taking into consideration the demeanor of the King at the said court, have notwithstanding resolved to try him once more whether he will own the court. And to that purpose: Ordered, that the Lord President do acquaint the King in case he shall continue contumacious that he is to expect no further time, and that the Lord President do therefore in the name of the court require his positive and final answer, and if he shall still persist in his obstinacy that the Lord President give command to the Clerk to read as followeth:

> Charles Stuart, King of England, you are accused on the behalf of the people of England of divers high crimes and treasons, which charge hath been read unto you. The court now requires you to give your final and positive answer by way of confession or denial of the charge.

Nevertheless, if the King should submit to answer and desire a copy of his charge, that it be granted him by the Lord President, notwithstanding giving him to know that the court might in justice forthwith proceed to judgment for his former contumacy and failure to answer, and that he be required to give his answer to the said charge the next day at 1 of the clock in the afternoon.

Whereupon the court adjourned to Westminster Hall forthwith.

The King's Trial Continues

A contemporary published transcript of the third day of the trial in Westminster Hall, seventy-three commissioners present

Oyez made. Silence commanded. The court called: seventy-three persons present. The King comes in with his guard, looks with an austere countenance upon the court, and sits down.

The second oyez made and silence commanded.

Mr. Cook, Solicitor General: May it please your lordship, my Lord President. This is now the third time that by the great grace and favor of this High Court the Prisoner hath been brought to the Bar before any issue joined in the cause. My lord, I did at the first court exhibit a charge against him containing the highest treason that ever was wrought upon the Theater of

England: that a King of England trusted to keep the law, that had taken an oath so to do, that had tribute paid him for that end, should be guilty of a wicked design [to] subvert and destroy our laws and introduce an arbitrary and tyrannical government in defiance of the Parliament and their authority, [and to] set up his standard for war against his Parliament and people. And I did humbly pray in the behalf of the people of England that he might speedily be required to make an answer to the charge.

But, my lord, instead of making any answer, he did then dispute the authority of this High Court. Your lordship was pleased to give him a further day to consider and to put in his answer, which day being yesterday I did humbly move that he might be required to give a direct and positive answer, either by denying or confession of it. But, my lord, he was then pleased for to demur to the jurisdiction of the court, which the court did then overrule and command him to give a direct and positive answer. My lord, besides this great delay of justice, I shall now humbly move your lordship for speedy judgment against him. My lord, I might press your lordship upon the whole that—according to the known rules of the law of the land—that if a prisoner shall stand as contumacious in contempt and shall not put in an issuable plea, Guilty or Not Guilty of the charge given against him, whereby he may come to a fair trial, that as by an implicit confession it may be taken as confessed, as it hath been done to those who have deserved more favor than the Prisoner at the Bar has done.

But besides, my lord, I shall humbly press your lordship upon the whole fact. The House of Commons, the supreme authority and jurisdiction of the kingdom, they have declared that it is notorious that the matter of the charge is true—as it is in truth, my lord, as clear as crystal and as the sun that shines at noonday—which if your lordship and the court be not satisfied in, I have notwithstanding on the people of England's behalf several witnesses to produce. And therefore I do humbly pray—and yet, I must confess, it is not so much I as the innocent blood that hath been shed, the cry whereof is very great for justice and judgment—and therefore I do humbly pray that speedy judgment be performed against the Prisoner at the Bar.

Lord President: Sir, you have heard what is moved by the Counsel on the behalf of the kingdom against you. Sir, you may well remember—and if you do not, the court cannot forget—what dilatory dealings the court hath found at your hands. You were pleased to propound some questions; you have had your resolutions upon them. You were told over and over again that the court did affirm their own jurisdiction, that it was not for you nor any other man to dispute the jurisdiction of the supreme and highest authority of England, from which there is no appeal and touching which there must be no dispute. Yet you did persist in such carriage as you gave no manner of obedience, nor did you acknowledge any authority in them nor [in] the high court [i.e., the Commons] that constituted this court of justice.

Sir, I must let you know from the court that they are very sensible of these delays of yours and that they ought not, being thus authorized by the supreme court of England, to be thus trifled withal, and that they might in justice—if they pleased, and according to the rules of justice—take advantage of these delays and proceed to pronounce judgment against you. Yet nevertheless they are pleased to give direction, and on their behalf I do require you, that you make a positive answer unto this charge that is against you. Sir, in plain terms—for justice knows no respect of persons—you are to give your positive and final answer in plain English, whether you be Guilty or Not Guilty of these treasons laid to your charge.

The King after a little pause said: When I was here yesterday, I did desire to speak for the liberties of the people of England. I was interrupted. I desire to know yet whether I may speak freely or not.

Lord President: Sir, you have had the resolution of the court upon the like question the last day and you were told that having such a charge of so high a nature against you, your work was that you ought to acknowledge the jurisdiction of the court and to answer to your charge. Sir, if you answer to your charge—which the court gives you leave now to do, though they might have taken the advantage of your contempt—yet if you be able to answer to your charge, when you have once answered you shall be heard at large make the best defense you can. But, sir, I must let you know from the court, as their commands, that you are not to be permitted to issue out into any other discourses till such time as you have given a positive answer concerning the matter that is charged upon you.

The King: For the charge, I value it not a rush. It is the liberty of the people of England that I stand for. For me to acknowledge a new court that I never heard of before—I that am your King, that should be an example to all the people of England for to uphold justice, to maintain the old laws—indeed I do not know how to do it. You spoke very well the first day that I came here (on Saturday) of the obligations that I had laid upon me by God to the maintenance of the liberties of my people. The same obligation you spake of I do acknowledge to God that I owe to Him and to my people to defend as much as in me lies the ancient laws of the kingdom. Therefore, until that I may know that this is not against the fundamental laws of the kingdom, by your favor, I can put in no particular charge (*this is as the King expressed, but I supposed he meant "answer"*). If you will give me time, I will show you my reasons why I cannot do it. And this—

Here being interrupted, he said: By your favor, you ought not to interrupt me. How I came here, I know not—there's no law for it, to make your King your prisoner. I was in a treaty upon the public faith of the kingdom. That was [with] the known—two Houses of Parliament that was the representative of the kingdom. And when that I had almost made an end of the treaty, then I was hurried away and brought hither, and therefore—

Here the Lord President said: Sir, you must know the pleasure of the court.

The King: By your favor, sir—

Lord President: Nay, sir, by your favor, you may not be permitted to fall into those discourses. You appear as a delinquent. You have not acknowledged the authority of the court. The court craves it not of you, but once more they command you to give your positive answer—Clerk, do your duty.

The King: Duty, sir!

The Clerk reads: Charles Stuart, King of England, you are accused in the behalf of the Commons of England of divers high crimes and treasons, which charge hath been read unto you. The court now requires you to give your positive and final answer by way of confession or denial of the charge.

The King: Sir, I say again to you, so that I might give satisfaction to the people of England of the clearness of my proceedings—not by way of answer, not in this way, but to satisfy them that I have done nothing against that trust that hath been committed to me—I would do it. But to acknowledge a new court against their privileges, to alter the fundamental laws of the kingdom—sir, you must excuse me.

Lord President: Sir, this is the third time that you have publicly disowned this court and put an affront upon it. How far you have preserved the privileges of the people, your actions have spoke it. But truly, sir, men's intentions ought to be known by their actions. You have written your meaning in bloody characters throughout the whole kingdom. But, sir, you understand the pleasure of the court—Clerk, record the default—and gentlemen, you that took charge of the Prisoner, take him back again.

The King: I will only say this one word more to you. If it were only my own particular, I would not say any more nor interrupt you—

Lord President: Sir, you have heard the pleasure of the court, and you are—notwithstanding you will not understand it—to find that you are before a court of justice.

Then the King went forth with his guard and proclamation was made that all persons which had then appeared and had further to do at the court might depart into the Painted Chamber, to which place the court did forthwith adjourn and intended to meet in Westminster Hall by 10 of the clock the next morning.

Crier: God bless the Kingdom of England!

The Court Confers Privately

The commissioners decide to hear witnesses—meeting in the Painted Chamber, as reported in Phelps's Journal

The court according to their former adjournment from Westminster Hall came together from thence into the Painted Chamber

John Cook: An obscure lawyer with a reputation for religious and political radicalism, John Cook burst into national prominence in January 1649 when he was named Solicitor to the High Court and given responsibility for drawing up the charge against the King. A week later he assumed the mantle of chief prosecutor when the man originally chosen for the job claimed to be too sick to serve. Rewarded with judgeships under the Commonwealth, Cook proved himself to be an ardent republican, a dedicated proponent of legal reform, and a compassionate defender of the underprivileged. To Royalists, however, Cook would always be the hypocritical religious extremist who had murdered his King, much as he is portrayed in this German print, the background of which alludes to his execution in 1660. Cook went to his death courageously and quietly, sure to the last of the rightness of his cause. "We are not traitors, nor murderers, nor fanatics," he wrote shortly before his execution, "but true Christians and good Commonwealth men." Detail from an anonymous German engraving. By courtesy of the Department of Prints and Drawings, British Museum.

where they sat privately and ordered as followeth: Ordered, that no commissioner ought, or shall, depart from the court without the special leave of the said court.

This court took into consideration the managing of the business of the court this day in the hall and the King's refusal to answer (notwithstanding he had been three several times demanded and required thereunto) and have thereupon fully approved of what on the court's part had then passed, and resolved that notwithstanding the said contumacy of the King and refusal to plead (which in law amounts to a standing mute and tacit confession of the charge) and notwithstanding the notoriety of the fact charged, the court would nevertheless, however, examine witnesses for the further and clearer satisfaction of their own judgments and consciences, the manner of whose examination was referred to further consideration [at] the next sitting, and warrants were accordingly issued forth for summoning of witnesses.

The court adjourned itself till 9 of the clock tomorrow morning to this place.

Wednesday, 24 January 1649

House of Commons

The House this day only met and adjourned.

High Court of Justice

The court takes depositions—meeting in the Painted Chamber, forty-seven commissioners present

This day it was expected the High Court of Justice would have met in Westminster Hall about 10 of the clock, but at the time appointed one of the ushers by direction of the court (then sitting in the Painted Chamber) gave notice to the people there assembled that in regard the court was then upon the examination of witnesses in

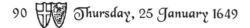

relation to present affairs in the Painted Chamber, they could not sit there, but all persons appointed to be there were to appear upon further summons.

Thursday, 25 January 1649

House of Commons

The House this day met again, and adjourned.

High Court of Justice

The evidence against the King—meeting in the Painted Chamber, thirty-two commissioners "with divers others" present, as reported in Phelps's Journal

The court ordered that the Marshal General of this Army or his deputy do bring forthwith Mr. Holder, prisoner at Whitehall, to the end that he may testify his knowledge of all such matters as shall be propounded unto him concerning the charge against the King.

Ordered, that the Dean's House in Westminster Abbey be provided and furnished for the lodging of the Lord President and his servants, guards and attendants, and a committee are appointed to take care hereof accordingly.

The witnesses sworn in open court and after examined by the committee appointed for that purpose the twenty-fourth instant, were now in open court called and their respective depositions were read to them, who did avow their said several depositions and affirm what was so read unto them respectively was true upon the oaths they had taken.

Mr. Holder being brought before this court according to the order of this day and his oath tendered unto him to give evidence to such matters as should be propounded unto him concerning the charge against the King, the said Mr. Holder desired to be spared from giving evidence against the King. Whereupon the commissioners, finding him already a prisoner and perceiving that the questions intended to be asked him tended to accuse himself, thought fit to waive his examination and remanded him (and accordingly did so) to the prison from whence he was brought.

A representative sampling of the thirty-two depositions heard in open court

William Cuthbert of Patrington in Holderness, gentleman, aged 42 years or thereabouts, sworn and examined, saith that he (this deponent), living at Hull Bridge, near Beverley, in July 1642 did then hear that forces were raised, about three thousand foot, for the King's Guard under Sir Robert Strickland. And this deponent further saith that about the second of July, 1642, he saw a troop of horse come to Beverley, being the Lord's day, about 4 or 5 of the clock in the afternoon, called the Prince's Troop, Mr. James Nelthorpe being then mayor of the said town. And this deponent further saith that he did see that afternoon the said troop march from Beverley aforesaid into Holderness, where they received ammunition brought up by the River of Humber unto them.

And this deponent further saith that the same night, being Sunday, there came about three hundred foot soldiers, said to be Sir Robert Strickland's regiment under the command of Lieutenant Colonel Duncombe and called the King's Guard, unto this deponent's house, called Hull Bridge, near Beverley, about midnight, and broke open, entered and possessed themselves of the said house; and that the Earl of Newport, the Earl of Carnarvon, and divers others came that night thither to the said forces; and that the same night (as this deponent was then informed) Sir Thomas Gower, then High Sheriff of the said county, came thither and left there a warrant for staying all provisions from going to Hull to Sir John Hotham, which said warrant was then delivered to this deponent, being Constable, by Lieutenant Colonel Duncombe.

And this deponent further saith that he was by the said forces put out of his house and did with his family go to Beverley; and after that (the Thursday following, to this deponent's best remembrance) he did see the King come to Beverley to the Lady Gee's house there, where he (this deponent) did often see the King with Prince Charles and the Duke of York; and that the trained bands were then raised in Holderness, who were raised (as was generally reported) by the King's command.

And this deponent further saith that the night after the said forces had possessed themselves of this deponent's house, Colonel Legard's house was plundered by them, being upon a Monday, which aforesaid entry of this deponent's house was the first act of hostility that was committed in those parts.

And this deponent further saith that after the said Sir Robert Strickland's said company was gone from Hull Bridge, having continued there about ten days, there then came to the said house Colonel Wyvill with about seven hundred foot soldiers, who then took up his quarters at Hull Bridge aforesaid.

And this deponent further saith that the General's name of the said forces that were there and raised as aforesaid was the Earl of Lindsey, and that this deponent was brought before him (the said General) in the name of the King's Lord General for holding intelligence with Sir John Hotham, then Governor of Hull, and because it was then informed to the said General that he (this deponent) had provisions of corn to send over unto Ireland, which he (this deponent) was forbidden by the said General to send unto Ireland or any place else without his or the King's direction or warrant first had in that behalf.

John Bennet of Harwood in the county of York, glover, sworn and examined, saith that he, being a soldier under the King's command the first day that the King's standard was set up at Nottingham (which was about the middle of summer last was six years), he (this examinant) did work at Nottingham; and that he did see the King within the Castle of Nottingham within two or three days after the said standard was so set up; and that the said standard did fly the same day that the King was in the said castle as aforesaid; and this deponent did hear that the King was at Nottingham the same day that the said standard was first set up, and before.

And this deponent further saith that he and the regiment of which he then was had their colors then given them; and Sir William Pennyman being the colonel of the said regiment, the said Sir William Pennyman was present with his said regiment at that time.

And this deponent further saith that there was then there the Earl of Lindsey's regiment, who had then their colors given them; and that the said Earl of Lindsey was then also proclaimed there the King's General; and that it was proclaimed then there likewise in the King's name at the head of every regiment that the said forces should fight against all that came to oppose the King or any of his followers, and in particular against the Earl of Essex, the Lord Brooke, and divers others; and that they, the said Earl of Essex and Lord Brooke and divers others, were then proclaimed traitors; and that the same proclamations were printed and dispersed by the officers of the regiments throughout every regiment.

And this deponent further saith that the said standard was advanced upon the highest tower of Nottingham Castle; and that he did see the King often in Nottingham at that time that the said forces continued at Nottingham as aforesaid, they continuing there for the space of one month; and that the drums for raising volunteers to fight under the King's command were then beaten all the said county over, and divers other forces were raised there. And this deponent further saith that he did take up arms under the King's command as aforesaid for fear of being plundered, Sir William Pennyman giving out that it were a good deed to fire the said town because they would not go forth in the King's service; and that this deponent's father did thereupon command him (this deponent) to take up arms as aforesaid; and that divers others (as they did confess) did then also take up arms for the King, for fear of being plundered.

And this deponent further saith that in or about the month of October 1642 he did see the King at Edgehill in Warwickshire, where he (sitting on horseback while his army was drawn up before him) did speak to the colonel of every regiment that passed by him that he would have them speak to their soldiers to encourage them to stand it and to fight against the Lord of Essex, the Lord Brooke, Sir William Waller, and Sir William Balfour.

And this deponent saith that he did see many slain at the fight at Edgehill, and that afterwards he did see a list brought in unto Oxford of the men which were slain in that fight, by which it was reported that there were slain 6,559 men.

And this deponent further saith, afterwards, in or about the month of November 1642, he did see the King in the head of his army at Hounslow Heath in Middlesex, Prince Rupert then standing by him. And he (this deponent) did then hear the King encourage several regiments of Welshmen (then being in the field) which had run away at Edgehill, saying unto them that he did hope they would regain their honor at Brentford which they had lost at Edgehill.

Robert Lacy of the town and county of Nottingham, painter, sworn and examined, deposeth that he (this deponent) in summertime in the year 1642, by order from my Lord Beaumont did paint the standard-pole which was set upon the top of the old tower of Nottingham Castle. And he further saith that he saw the King in the town of Nottingham divers times while the standard was up there and the flag flying, and the King did lie at the house of my lord of Clare in Nottingham town; and that he (this deponent) did then and there see the King many times.

Samuel Morgan of Wellington in the county of Salop, felt-maker, sworn and examined, deposeth that he (this deponent) upon a Sunday morning in Kineton Field saw the King upon the top of Edgehill in the head of the army some two hours before the fight, which happened after Michaelmas on a Sunday, the year 1642. And he (this deponent) saw many men killed on both sides in the same time and place.

And he further saith that in the year 1644 he saw the King in his army near Cropredy Bridge, where he saw the King light off his horse and draw up the body of his army in person himself.

James Williams of Ross in Herefordshire, shoemaker, sworn and examined, deposeth that he (this deponent) about October [in] the year 1642 saw the King in Kineton Field, below the hill in the field with his sword drawn in his hand, at which time and place there was a great fight and many killed on both sides.

And he further deposeth that he saw the King at Brentford on a Sunday in the forenoon, in November [in] the year above-said, while the King's army was in the said town and round about it.

John Pynneger of the parish of Heanor in the county of Derby, yeoman, aged 37 years or thereabouts, sworn and examined, saith that about August 1642 he (the deponent) saw the King's standard flying upon one of the towers of Nottingham Castle; and that upon the same day he saw the King in Thurland House, being the Earl of Clare's house in Nottingham, in the company of Prince Rupert, Sir John Digby, and other persons, both noblemen and others; and that the King had at the same time in the said town a train of artillery, and the said town was then full of the King's soldiers.

Samuel Lawson of Nottingham, maltster, aged 30 years or thereabouts, sworn and examined, saith that about August 1642 he (this deponent) saw the King's standard brought forth of Nottingham Castle, borne upon divers gentlemen's shoulders, who (as the report was) were noblemen; and he saw the same by them carried to the hill close adjoining to the castle with a herald before it, and there the said standard was erected with great shoutings, acclamations, and sound of drums and trumpets; and that when the said standard was so erected there was a proclamation made; and that he (this deponent) saw the King present at the erecting thereof.

And this deponent further saith that the said town was then full of the King's soldiers, of which some quartered in this deponent's house; and that when the King with his said forces went from the said town, the inhabitants of the said town were forced to pay a great sum of money to the King's army, being threatened that in case they should refuse to pay it the said town should be plundered.

Arthur Young, citizen and barber-surgeon of London, being aged 29 years or thereabouts, sworn and examined, saith that he (this deponent) was present at the fight at Edgehill between the King's army and the Parliament's in October 1642, and he did then see the King's standard advanced and flying in his army in the said fight. And that he (this deponent) did then take the King's said standard in that battle from the King's forces, which was afterwards taken from him by one Middleton who was afterwards made a colonel.

John Thomas of Llangollen in the county of Denbigh, husbandman, aged 25 years or thereabouts, sworn and examined, saith that he saw the King at Brentford in the county of Middlesex on a Saturday night at 12 of the clock soon after Edgehill Fight, attended with horse and foot soldiers, the King being then on horseback with his sword by his side. And this deponent then heard the King say to the said soldiers as he was riding through the said town, "Gentlemen, you lost your honor at Edgehill, I hope you will regain it again here"—or words to that effect. And this deponent further saith that there were some skirmishes between the King's army and the Parliament's army at the same time, both before and after the King spake the said words, and that many men were slain on both sides.

Richard Blomfield, citizen and weaver of London, aged 35 years or thereabouts, sworn and examined, saith that at the defeat of the Earl of Essex's army in Cornwall, he (this deponent) was there, it being at the latter end of the month of August or beginning of September 1644, at which time he saw the King at the head of his army near Fowey on horseback; and further saith that he did then see divers of the Lord of Essex's soldiers plundered, contrary to articles then lately made, near the person of the King.

William Jones of Usk in the county of Monmouth, husbandman, aged 22 years or thereabouts, sworn and examined saith that he (this deponent) did see the King within two miles of Naseby Field, the King then coming fromwards [i.e., away from] Harborough, marching in the head of his army towards Naseby Field where the fight was; and that he (this deponent) did then see the King ride up to the regiment which was Colonel St. George's, and there the deponent did hear the King ask the regiment whether they were willing to fight for him. To which the soldiers made an acclamation, crying "All! All!"

And this deponent further saith that he saw the King in Leicester with his forces, the same day that the King's forces had taken it from the Parliament's forces. And this deponent further saith that he saw the King in his army that besieged Gloucester at the time of the said siege.

Humphrey Browne of Whissendine in the county of Rutland, husbandman, aged 22 years or thereabouts, sworn and examined, saith that at such time as the town of Leicester was taken by the King's forces, being in or about June 1645, Newark Fort, in Leicester aforesaid, was surrendered to the King's forces upon composition that neither clothes nor money should be taken away from any of the soldiers of that fort which had so surrendered, nor any violence offered to them; and that as soon as the said fort was upon such composition so surrendered as aforesaid, the King's soldiers, contrary to the articles, fell upon the soldiers of the said fort, stripped, cut and wounded many of them; whereupon, one of the King's officers rebuking some of those that did so abuse the said Parliament's soldiers, this deponent did then hear the King reply, "I do not care if they cut them three times more, for they are mine enemies," or words to that effect;

and that the King was then on horseback in bright armor in the said town of Leicester.

John Vinson of Damerham in the county of Wilts, gentleman, sworn and examined, saith that he did see the King at the first Newbury Fight about the month of September 1643 in the head of his army, where this deponent did see many slain on both sides.

This deponent also saith that he did see the King at the second battle at Newbury about the month of November 1644, where the King was at the head of his army in complete armor with his sword drawn. And this deponent did then see the King lead up Colonel Thomas Howard's regiment of horse and did hear him make a speech to the soldiers in the head of that regiment to this effect, that is to say that the said regiment should stand to him that day for that his Crown lay upon the point of the sword, and if he lost that day, he lost his honor and his Crown forever. And that this deponent did see many slain on both sides at that battle.

This deponent further saith that he did see the King in the battle at Naseby Field in Northamptonshire on or about the month of June 1645, where the King was then completely armed with back, breast and helmet, and had his sword drawn, [and] where the King himself, after his party was routed, did rally up the horse and caused them to stand. And at that time this deponent did see many slain on both sides.

Thomas Rawlins of Hanslope in the county of Bucks, gentleman, sworn and examined, saith that he did see the King near Fowey in Cornwall in or about the month of July 1644 at the head of a party of horse; and this deponent did see some soldiers plundered after the articles of agreement made between the King's army and the Parliament's forces, which soldiers were so plundered by the King's party not far distant from the person of the King.

The examination of Henry Gooch of Gray's Inn in the county of Middlesex, gentleman, sworn and examined. This deponent saith that upon or about the thirtieth day of September last, he (this deponent) was in the Isle of Wight and had access unto, and discourse with, the King by the means of the Lord Marquis of Hertford and Commissary Morgan, where this deponent told the King that His

Majesty had many friends and that since His Majesty was pleased to justify the Parliament's first taking up arms, the most of the Presbyterian party, both soldiers and others, would stick close to him. To which the King answered thus, that he would have all his old friends know that though for the present he was contented to give the Parliament leave to call their own war what they pleased, yet that he neither did at that time, nor ever should, decline the justice of his own cause.

And this deponent told the King that his business was much retarded, and that neither Colonel Thomas nor any other could proceed to action through want of commission. The King answered that he, being upon a treaty, would not dishonor himself, but that if he (this deponent) would take the pains to go over to the Prince his son (who had full authority from him), he (the said deponent) or any for him should receive whatsoever commissions should be desired, and to that purpose he would appoint the Marquis of Hertford to write to his son in his name, and was pleased to express much of joy and affection that his good subjects would engage themselves for his restoration.

The court hears its last testimony and reaches a verdict—afternoon meeting with forty-six commissioners present, as reported in Phelps's Journal

Richard Price of London, scrivener, was produced a witness to the charge against the King, who being sworn and examined saith that upon occasion of some tampering by the King's agents with the Independents in and about London to draw them from the Parliament's cause to the King's party, and this being discovered by some of those so tampered with unto sundry members of the Committee of Safety who directed a carrying on of a seeming compliance with the King, he (this deponent) did travel to Oxford in January 1644 having a safe-conduct under the King's hand and seal, which he (this deponent) knoweth to be so, for that the King did own it when he was told that this deponent was the man that came to Oxford with that safe-conduct.

And this deponent also saith that after sundry meetings between him and the Earl of Bristol about the drawing of the Independents unto the King's cause against the Parliament, the substance of the discourse at which meetings (the said Earl told this deponent) was communicated to the King, he (this deponent) was by the said Earl brought to the King to confer further about that business, where the King declared that he was very sensible that the Independents had been the most active men in the kingdom for the Parliament against him, and thereupon persuaded this deponent to use all means to expedite their turning to him and his cause. And for their better encouragement, the King promised in the word of a King that if they (the Independents) would turn to him and be active for him against the Parliament as they had been active for them against him, then he would grant them whatsoever freedom they would desire. And the King did then refer this deponent unto the Earl of Bristol for the further prosecuting of the said business.

And the said Earl thereupon (this deponent being withdrawn from the King) did declare unto this deponent, and willed him to impart the same unto the Independents for their better encouragement, that the King's affairs prospered well in Ireland; that the Irish subjects had given the rebels (meaning the Parliament's forces) a great defeat; that the King had sent the Lord Byron with a small party towards Cheshire, and that he was greatly multiplied and had a considerable army and was then before Nantwich and would be strengthened with more soldiers out of Ireland, which were come and expected daily. And when this deponent was to depart out of Oxford, four safe-conducts, with blanks in them for the inserting of what names this deponent pleased, were delivered to him under the King's hand and seal. And one Ogle was sent out of Oxford with this deponent to treat about the delivering up of Aylesbury to the King, it being then a garrison for the Parliament, and at the same time Oxford was a garrison for the King.

Several papers and letters of the King's, under his own hand and of his own writing, and other papers, are produced and read in open court. Mr. Thomas Chaloner also reporteth several papers and letters of the King's writing and under the King's own hand. After which the court sat private.

The court, taking into consideration the whole matter in charge against the King, passed these votes following as preparatory to the sentence against the King, but ordered that they should not be binding finally to conclude the court:

Resolved upon the whole matter, that this court will proceed to sentence of condemnation against Charles Stuart, King of England.

Resolved, that the condemnation of the King shall be for a tyrant, traitor, and murderer; that the condemnation of the King shall be likewise for being a public enemy to the Commonwealth of England; that this condemnation shall extend to death.

The court, being then moved concerning the deposition and deprivation of the King before and in order to that part of his sentence which concerned his execution, thought fit to defer the consideration thereof to some other time, and ordered the draft of a sentence grounded upon the said votes to be accordingly prepared by Mr. Scot, Mr. Marten, Colonel Harrison, Mr. Lisle, Mr. Say, Commissary General Ireton, and Mr. Love, or any three of them, with a blank for the manner of his death.

Ordered, that the members of this court who are in and about London and are not now present be summoned to attend the service of this court tomorrow at 1 of the clock in the afternoon, for whom summons were issued forth accordingly.

The court adjourned itself till the morrow at 1 of the clock in the afternoon.

Friday, 26 January 1649

House of Commons

From the Journals of the House of Commons

Mr. Speaker informed the House that addresses have been made to him by some agents from the Ambassadors of the States-General of Holland, who certified [to] him that Ambassadors from the States in Holland were at Greenwich and desired him to acquaint this House therewith. Ordered, that the Master of the Ceremonies be appointed to wait on the Ambassadors at Greenwich and to bring them up to the City of London with all civil respects.

The Great Seal of the Commonwealth: Every revolution needs new symbols of legitimacy. The Great Seal of England, whose presence gave legal validity to the chief documents of state, traditionally showed an image of the King enthroned and, on its reverse, an image of the King armed and riding on horseback. The King's conquerors redesigned the seal to be a statement of their own rampant republicanism: it shows the House of Commons in session and, on its reverse, a map of England, Ireland, and Wales. The design was approved by the House of Commons on 9 January, with funds for its engraving appropriated on the twenty-sixth; Thomas Simon, the engraver, worked quickly, delivering a rough rendering of the new seal less than two weeks later. The Second Seal of the Commonwealth, reproduced here, follows the same design but is more carefully finished. Engraved by Simon, it was adopted in 1651, which by the Commonwealth's count was "The Third Year of Freedom by God's Blessing Restored." Department of Manuscripts, British Library. Reproduced by permission of the British Library.

Mr. Lisle reports an act for settling proceedings in courts of justice, which was this day read the first and second time, and upon the question ordered to be engrossed.

Ordered, that Thomas Simon be hereby authorized to engrave a seal according to the form formerly directed. Ordered, that Thomas Simon shall have the sum of £200 for engraving the said Great Seal and for the materials thereof.

Ordered, that the committee for considering the letters and papers of the Scots commissioners do examine whether the same are printed and whether the same were done by the direction of the Scots commissioners or by whom, and report it to this House.

High Court of Justice

The sentence is drafted—private meeting in the Painted Chamber, sixty-two commissioners present, as reported in Phelps's Journal

Here the court sat private.

The draft of a sentence against the King is according to the votes of the twenty-fifth instant prepared, and after several readings, debates, and amendments by the court thereupon: Resolved, that this court do agree to the sentence now read; that the said sentence shall be engrossed; that the King be brought to Westminster tomorrow to receive his sentence.

The court adjourned itself till the morrow at 10 of the clock in the morning to this place, the court giving notice that they then intended to adjourn from thence to Westminster Hall.

Saturday, 27 January 1649

High Court of Justice

Preliminary meeting in the Painted Chamber, sixty-eight commissioners present, as reported in Phelps's Journal

The sentence agreed on and ordered by this court [the] twenty-sixth instant to be engrossed, being accordingly engrossed, was read.

Resolved, that the sentence now read shall be the sentence of this court for the condemnation of the King, which shall be read and published in Westminster Hall this day.

The court hereupon considered of certain instructions for the Lord President to manage the business of this day in Westminster Hall, and ordered that the Lord President do manage what discourse shall happen between him and the King according to his discretion with the advice of his two assistants; that in case the King shall still persist in excepting against the court's jurisdiction, to let him know that the court do still affirm their jurisdiction; that in case the King shall submit to the jurisdiction of the court and pray a copy of the charge, that then the court do withdraw and advise; that in case the King shall move anything else worth the court's consideration, that the Lord President, upon advice of his said assistants, do give order for the court's withdrawing to advise; that in case the King shall not submit to answer and there happen no such cause of withdrawing, that then the Lord President do command the sentence to be read, but that the Lord President should hear the King say what he would before the sentence, and not after.

And thereupon it being further moved whether the Lord President should use any discourses or speeches to the King, as in the case of other prisoners to be condemned was usual before the publishing of the sentence, [he] received general directions to do therein as he should see cause and to press what he should conceive most seasonable and suitable to the occasion. And it was further directed that after the reading of the sentence the Lord President should declare that the same was the sentence, judgment, and resolution of the whole court, and that the commissioners should thereupon signify their consent by standing up.

The court forthwith adjourned itself to Westminster Hall.

The King is sentenced—Westminster Hall, sixty-seven commissioners present, as reported in Phelps's Journal

The Lord President and the rest of the commissioners come together from the Painted Chamber to Westminster Hall according to their adjournment, and take their seats there, as formerly. And three proclamations being made for attendance and silence, the court is called.

The Prisoner is brought to the Bar, and proclamation is again (as formerly) made for silence, and the Captain of the Guard ordered to take into his custody all such as should disturb the court.

The President stood up with an intention of address to the people and not to the Prisoner who had so often declined the jurisdiction of the court, which the Prisoner observing, moved he might be heard before judgment [was] given, whereof he received assurance from the court and that he should be heard after he had heard them first.

Whereupon the President proceeded and remembered the great assembly then present of what had formerly passed betwixt the court and the Prisoner: the charge against him in the name of the people of England exhibited to them, being a court constituted by the supreme authority of England; his refusal three several days and times to own them as a court or to answer to the matter of his charge; his thrice-recorded contumacy, and other his contempts and defaults in the precedent courts. Upon which the court then declared that they might not be wanting to themselves or to the trust reposed in them and that no man's willfulness ought to serve him to prevent justice, and that they had therefore thought fit to take the substance of what had passed into their serious consideration, to wit, the charge and the Prisoner's contumacy, and the confession which in law doth arise upon that contumacy, the notoriety of the fact charged, and other circumstances material in the cause, and upon the whole matter had resolved and agreed upon a sentence then ready to be pronounced against the Prisoner. But that in regard of his desire to be further heard, they were ready to hear him as to anything material which he would offer to their consideration, before the sentence [was] given, relating to the defense of himself concerning the matter charged; and did then signify so much to the Prisoner, who made use of that leave given only to protest his respects to the peace of the kingdom and liberty of the subject, and to say that the same made him at last to desire, that having somewhat to say that concerned both, he might before the sentence [was] given be heard in the Painted Chamber before the Lords and Commons, saying it was fit to be heard if it were reason which he should offer, whereof they were judges.

And pressing that point much, he was forthwith answered by the court and told: that that which he had moved was a declining of the jurisdiction of the court, whereof he had caution frequently before given him; that it sounded to further delay, of which he had been too much guilty; that the court being founded (as often had been said) upon the authority of the Commons of England, in whom rested the supreme jurisdiction, the motion tended to set up another or a coordinate jurisdiction in derogation of the power whereby the court sat and to the manifest delay of their justice, in which regard he was told they might forthwith proceed to sentence. Yet for his further satisfaction of the entire pleasure and judgment of the court upon what he had then said, he was told, and accordingly it was declared, that the court would withdraw half an hour.

The Prisoner by command being withdrawn, the court made their recess into the room called the Court of Wards, considered of the Prisoner's motion, and gave the President direction to declare their dissent thereto and to proceed to the sentence.

The court being again seated and the Prisoner returned, [he] was according to their direction informed that he had in effect received his answer before the court withdrew, and that their judgment was (as to his motion) the same [as had been] to him before declared, that the court acted and were judges appointed by the highest authority, and that judges were not to delay no more than to deny justice; that they were good words in the Great Old Charter of England, "To no one will we refuse, to no one will we sell, to no one will we delay justice or right" [paraphrasing Magna Carta, cap. 40/29]; that their duty called upon them to avoid further delays and to proceed to judgment, which was their unanimous resolution. Unto which the Prisoner replied and insisted upon his former desires, confessing a delay, but that it was important for the peace of the kingdom, and therefore pressed again with much earnestness to be heard before the Lords and Commons.

In answer whereto he was told by the court that they had fully before considered of his proposal and must give him the same answer to his renewed desires, and that they were ready to proceed to sentence if he had nothing more to say. Whereunto he subjoined he had no more to say, but desired that might be entered which he had said.

Hereupon after some discourse used by the President for vindicating the Parliament's justice, explaining the nature of the crimes of which the Prisoner stood charged and for which he was to be condemned, and by way of exhortation of the Prisoner to a serious repentance for his high transgressions against God and the people and to prepare for his eternal condition, the sentence formerly agreed upon and put down in parchment writing (oyez being first made for silence) was by the court's command solemnly pronounced and given, the tenor whereof followeth:

Whereas the Commons of England assembled in Parliament have by their late act entitled *An Act of the Commons of England Assembled in Parliament, for Erecting of an High Court of Justice for the Trying and Judging of Charles Stuart, King of England,* authorized and constituted us an High Court of Justice for the trying and judging of the said Charles Stuart for the crimes and treasons in the said act mentioned, by virtue whereof the said Charles Stuart hath been three several times convened before this High Court, where the first day, being Saturday, the twentieth of January instant, in pursuance of the said act a charge of High Treason and other high crimes was in the behalf of the people of England exhibited against him and read openly unto him, wherein he was charged that he (the said Charles Stuart) being admitted King of England and therein trusted with a limited power to govern by and according to the law of the land and not otherwise, and by his trust, oath, and office being obliged to use the power committed to him for the good and benefit of the people and for the preservation of their rights and liberties, yet nevertheless out of a wicked design to erect and uphold in himself an unlimited and tyrannical power to rule according to his will and to overthrow the rights and liberties of the people, and to take away and make void the foundations thereof and of all redress and remedy of misgovernment, which by the fundamental constitutions of this kingdom were reserved on the people's behalf in the right and power of frequent and successive Parliaments or National Meetings in Council, he (the said Charles Stuart) for accomplishment of such his designs and for the protecting of himself and his adherents in his and their wicked practices to the same end hath traitorously and maliciously levied war against the present Parliament and people therein represented, as (with the circumstances of time and place) is in the said charge more particularly set forth; and that he hath thereby caused and procured many thousands of the free people of this nation to

be slain, and by divisions, parties, and insurrections within
this land, by invasions from foreign parts, endeavored and
procured by him, and by many other evil ways and means,
he (the said Charles Stuart) hath not only maintained and
carried on the said war both by sea and land but also hath
renewed, or caused to be renewed, the said war against the
Parliament and good people of this nation in this present
year 1648/49 in several counties and places in this kingdom
in the charge specified; and that he hath for that purpose
given his commission to his son the Prince and others whereby, besides multitudes of other persons, many such as were
by the Parliament entrusted and employed for the safety of
this nation being by him or his agents corrupted to the
betraying of their trust and revolting from the Parliament
have had entertainment and commission for the continuing
and renewing of the war and hostility against the said
Parliament and people; and that by the said cruel and unnatural war so levied, continued, and renewed, much innocent
blood of the free people of this nation hath been spilt, many
families undone, the public treasure wasted, trade obstructed
and miserably decayed, vast expense and damage to the
nation incurred, and many parts of the land spoiled, some of
them even to desolation; and that he still continues his commission to his said son and other rebels and revolters, both
English and foreigners, and to the Earl of Ormonde and to
the Irish rebels and revolters associated with him, from
whom further invasions upon this land are threatened by his
procurement and on his behalf; and that all the said wicked
designs, wars, and evil practices of him (the said Charles
Stuart) were still carried on for the advancement and
upholding of the personal interest of will, power, and pretended prerogative to himself and his family, against the
public interest, common right, liberty, justice, and peace of
the people of this nation; and that he thereby hath been and
is the occasioner, author, and continuer of the said unnatural,
cruel and bloody wars, and therein guilty of all the treasons,
murders, rapines, burnings, spoils, desolations, damage, and
mischief to this nation, acted and committed in the said wars
or occasioned thereby.

Whereupon the proceedings and judgment of this court were prayed against him as a tyrant, traitor, and murderer, and public enemy to the Commonwealth, as by the said charge more fully appeareth. To which charge, being read unto him as aforesaid, he (the said Charles Stuart) was required to give his answer, but he refused so to do. And upon Monday, the twenty-second day of January instant, being again brought before this court and there required to answer directly to the said charge, he still refused so to do, whereupon his default and contumacy was entered. And the next day, being the third time brought before the court, judgment was then prayed against him on the behalf of the people of England for his contumacy and for the matters contained against him in the said charge, as taking the same for confessed in regard of his refusing to answer thereto, yet notwithstanding this court (not willing to take advantage of his contempt) did once more require him to answer to the said charge, but he again refused so to do. Upon which his several defaults, this court might justly have proceeded to judgment against him both for his contumacy and the matters of the charge, taking the same for confessed as aforesaid. Yet nevertheless, this court, for their own clearer information and further satisfaction, have thought fit to examine witnesses upon oath and take notice of other evidences touching the matters contained in the said charge, which accordingly they have done.

Now, therefore, upon serious and mature deliberation of the premises and consideration had of the notoriety of the matters of fact charged upon him as aforesaid, this court is in judgment and conscience satisfied that he (the said Charles Stuart) is guilty of levying war against the said Parliament and people, and [of] maintaining and continuing the same, for which in the said charge he stands accused. And by the general course of his government, counsels, and practices, before and since this Parliament began (which have been and are notorious and public, and the effects whereof remain abundantly upon record), this court is fully satisfied in their judgments and consciences that he hath been and is guilty of the wicked designs and endeavors in the said charge set forth; and that the said war hath been levied, maintained, and continued by him as aforesaid, in prosecution and for accomplishment of the said designs; and that he hath been and is the occasioner, author, and continuer of the said unnatural, cruel and bloody wars, and therein guilty of High Treason and of the murders, rapines, burnings, spoils, desolations, damage, and mischief to this nation acted and committed in the said war and occasioned thereby.

For all which treasons and crimes, this court doth adjudge that he, the said Charles Stuart, as a tyrant, traitor, murderer, and public enemy to the good people of this nation, shall be put to death by the severing of his head from his body.

This sentence being read, the President spake as followeth: "The sentence now read and published is the act, sentence, judgment and resolution of the whole court," whereupon the whole court stood up and owned it.

The Prisoner being withdrawn, the court adjourned itself forthwith into the Painted Chamber.

The court meets privately, sixty-four commissioners present, as reported in Phelps's Journal

The court being seated in the Painted Chamber according to adjournment from Westminster Hall aforesaid, Sir Hardress Waller, Colonel Harrison, Commissary General Ireton, Colonel Deane, and Colonel Okey are appointed to consider of the time and place for the execution of the sentence against the King.

And then the court adjourned itself till Monday morning at 8 of the clock to this place.

Another Account of the King's Sentencing

A contemporary transcript of the last day of the trial in Westminster Hall, with later interpolations by the royalist John Nalson given in italics

The King being come in his wonted posture with his hat on, some of the soldiers began to call for "Justice! Justice!" and "Execution!"

But silence being commanded, His Majesty began: "I desire a word to be heard a little, and I hope I shall give no occasion of interruption."

Bradshaw saucily answered: You may answer in your time. Hear the court first.

His Majesty patiently replied: If it please you, sir, I desire to be heard, and I shall not give any occasion of interruption, and it is only in a word. A sudden judgment—

Bradshaw: Sir, you shall be heard in due time, but you are to hear the court first.

King: Sir, I desire it. It will be in order to what I believe the court will say. And therefore, sir, a hasty judgment is not so soon recalled—

Bradshaw: Sir, you shall be heard before the judgment be given, and in the meantime you may forbear.

King: Well, sir, shall I be heard before the judgment be given?

Bradshaw: Gentlemen, it is well known to all or most of you here present that the Prisoner at the Bar hath been several times convened and brought before this court to make answer to a charge of treason and other high crimes exhibited against him in the name of the people of England—*Here a lady interposed saying "not half the people!" but was silenced with threats*—to which charge—being required to answer—he hath been so far from obeying the commands of the court by submitting to their justice as he began to take upon him to offer reasoning and debate unto the authority of the court and to the highest court that appointed them to try and judge him. But being overruled in that and required to make his answer, he was still pleased to continue contumacious, and to refuse to submit to answer. Hereupon the court—that they might not be wanting to themselves nor [to] the trust reposed in them, nor that any man's willfulness prevent justice—they have thought fit to take the matter into their consideration. They have considered of the charge. They have considered of the contumacy, and of that confession which in law doth arise upon that contumacy. They have likewise considered of the notoriety of the fact charged upon the Prisoner. And upon the whole matter they are resolved and are agreed upon a sentence to be pronounced against this Prisoner. But in respect he doth desire to be heard before the sentence be read and pronounced, the court hath resolved that they will hear him.

Yet, sir, thus much I must tell you beforehand, which you have been minded of at other courts. That if that which you have to say be to offer any debate concerning the jurisdiction, you are not to be heard in it. You have offered it formerly, and you have struck at the root—that is, [at] the power and supreme authority of the Commons of England, which this court will not admit a debate of, and which indeed it is an irrational thing in them to do, being a court that acts upon authority derived from them. But, sir, if you have anything to say in defense of yourself concerning the matter charged, the court hath given me in command to let you know they will hear you.

King: Since I see that you will not hear anything of debate concerning that which I confess I thought most material for the peace of the kingdom and for the liberty of the subject, I shall waive it—I shall speak nothing to it. But only I must tell you that this many a day all things have been taken away from me, but that that I call dearer to me than my life, which is my conscience and my honor. And if I had a respect to my life more than [to] the peace of the kingdom and liberty of the subject, certainly I should have made a particular defense for myself, for by that (at leastwise) I might have delayed an ugly sentence which I believe will pass upon me. Therefore certainly, sir, as a man that hath some understanding, some knowledge of the world, if that my true zeal to my country had not overborne the care that I have for my own preservation, I should have gone another way to work than that I have done.

Now, sir, I conceive that an hasty sentence once passed may sooner be repented of than recalled. And truly, the selfsame desire that I have for the peace of the kingdom and the liberty of the subject, more than my own particular ends, makes me now at last desire that I—having something to say that concerns both, before sentence be given—that I may be heard in the Painted Chamber before the Lords and Commons. This delay cannot be prejudicial unto you, whatsoever I say. If that I say [hath] no reason, those that hear me must be judges; I cannot be judge of that that I have. If it be reason and really for the welfare of the kingdom and the liberty of the subject, I am sure on it, it is very well worth the hearing. Therefore I do conjure you, as you love that that you pretend—I hope it is real—the liberty of the subject, the peace of the kingdom, that you will grant me this hearing before any sentence be passed. I only desire this, that you will take this into your consideration—it may be you have not heard of it beforehand. If you will, I will retire and you may think of it. But if I cannot get this liberty, I do protest that these fair shows of liberty and peace are pure shows, and that you will not hear your King.

Bradshaw: Sir, you have now spoken?

King: Yes, sir.

Bradshaw: And this that you have said is a further declining of the jurisdiction of this court, which was the thing wherein you were limited before—

King: Pray excuse me, sir, for my interruption, because you mistake me. It is not a declining of it. You do judge me before you hear me speak. I say I will not—I do not—decline it, though I cannot acknowledge the jurisdiction of the court. Yet, sir, in this give me leave to say I would do it, though I did not acknowledge it. In this I do protest, it is not the declining of it, since I say if that I do say anything but that that is for the peace of the kingdom and the liberty of the subject, then the shame is mine. Now I desire that you will take this into your consideration. If you will, I will withdraw.

Bradshaw: Sir, this is not altogether new that you have moved to us, not altogether new to us, though the first time in person you have offered it to the court. Sir, you say you do not decline the jurisdiction of the court?

King: Not in this that I have said.

Bradshaw: I understand you well, sir, but nevertheless that which you have offered seems to be contrary to that saying of yours, for the court are ready to give a sentence. It is not, as you say, that they will not hear their King, for they have been ready to hear you. They have patiently waited your pleasure for three courts together to hear what you would say to the people's charge against you, to which you have not vouchsafed to give any answer at all. Sir, this tends to a further delay. Truly, sir, such delays as these neither may the kingdom nor justice well bear. You have had three several days to have offered in this kind what you would have pleased. This court is founded upon that authority of the Commons of England, in whom rests the supreme jurisdiction. That which you now tender is to have another jurisdiction and a coordinate jurisdiction. I know very well you express yourself, sir, that notwithstanding that you would offer to the Lords and Commons in the Painted Chamber, yet nevertheless you would proceed on here—I did hear you say so. But, sir, that you would offer there—whatever it is—must needs be in delay of the justice here; so as if this court be resolved and prepared for the sentence, this that you offer they are not bound to grant. But, sir, according to that you seem to desire, and because you shall know the further pleasure of the court upon that which you have moved, the court will withdraw for a time.

This he did to prevent the disturbance of their scene by one of their own members, Colonel John Downes, who could not stifle the reluctance of his conscience when he saw His Majesty press so earnestly for a short hearing, but declaring himself unsatisfied forced them to yield to the King's request.

King: Shall I withdraw?

Bradshaw: Sir, you shall know the pleasure of the court presently. The court withdraws for half an hour into the Court of Wards. Sergeant at Arms, the court gives command that the Prisoner be withdrawn and they give order for his return again.

Then withdrawing into the chamber of the Court of Wards, their business was not to consider His Majesty's desire, but to chide Downes, and with reproaches and threats to harden him to go through the remainder of their villainy with them. Which done, they returned, and being seated, Bradshaw commanded: "Sergeant at Arms, send for your Prisoner," who being come, Bradshaw proceeded.

Bradshaw: Sir, you were pleased to make a motion here to the court to offer a desire of yours touching the propounding of somewhat to the Lords and Commons in the Painted Chamber for the peace of the kingdom. Sir, you did in effect receive an answer before the court adjourned. Truly, sir, their withdrawing and adjournment was merely as a matter of form, for it did not seem to them that there was any difficulty in the thing. They have considered of what you have moved, and have considered of their own authority, which is founded—as hath been often said—upon the supreme authority of the Commons of England assembled in Parliament. The court acts accordingly to their commission.

Sir, the return I have to you from the court is this: that they have been too much delayed by you already, and this that you now offer hath occasioned some little further delay; and they are judges appointed by the highest authority, and judges are no more to delay than they are to deny justice. They are good words in the Great Old Charter of England, "To no one will we refuse, to no one will we sell, to no one will we delay justice" [paraphrasing Magna Carta, cap. 40/29]. There must be no delay. But the truth is, sir—and so every man here observes it—that you have much delayed them in your contempt and default, for which they might long since have proceeded to judgment against you. And notwithstanding what you have offered, they are resolved to proceed to sentence and to judgment, and that is their unanimous resolution.

King: Sir, I know it is in vain for me to dispute—I am no Skeptic for to deny the power that you have. I know that you have power enough. Sir, I must confess I think it would have been for the kingdom's peace if you would have taken the pains to have shown the lawfulness of your power. For this delay that I have desired, I confess it is a delay. But it is a delay very important for the peace of the kingdom—for it is not my person that I look at alone, it is the kingdom's welfare and the kingdom's peace. It is an old sentence [i.e., maxim] that we should think on long before we resolve of great matters suddenly. Therefore, sir, I do say again, that I do put at your doors all the inconveniency of a hasty sentence. I confess I have been here now, I think, this week—this day eight days was the day I came here first. But a little delay of a day or two further may give peace, whereas a hasty judgment may bring on that trouble and perpetual inconveniency to the kingdom that the child that is unborn may repent it. And therefore again, out of the duty I owe to God and to my country, I do desire that I may be heard by the Lords and

Oliver Cromwell: In the official record of Charles's trial, Oliver Cromwell appears only as one of many commissioners, with powers no different from those of his fellows. In a sense, the enigmatic Lieutenant General of the Army was a latecomer to the proceedings, having decided to support them less than a month before they actually took place. Once that decision was made, however, his became the dominant voice in the court's private meetings, rallying supporters and bullying doubters to ensure the outcome. Of the fifty-nine commissioners who signed the death warrant, eight were Cromwell's relatives, including his son-in-law Henry Ireton. Several of the others, such as John Downes, later claimed that they signed out of sheer fear of him. Cromwell soon became Lord Protector of the new Commonwealth, but his elevation led Cook, Bradshaw, and other republicans to break with him amidst charges that he himself was assuming royalist airs. His death in 1658 set in motion the train of events that would restore the monarchy. Detail from a portrait by Robert Walker, ca. 1649. National Portrait Gallery, London. Reproduced by kind permission.

Commons in the Painted Chamber, or any other chamber that you will appoint me.

Bradshaw: You have been already answered to what you even now moved, being the same you moved before. [You had] the resolution and the judgment of the court in it. And the court now requires to know whether you have any more to say for yourself than you have said, before they proceed to sentence.

King: I say this, sir, that if you hear me—if you will give me but this delay—I doubt not but I shall give some satisfaction to you all here and to my people after that. And therefore I do require you—as you will answer it at the dreadful Day of Judgment—that you will consider it once again.

Bradshaw: Sir, I have received direction from the court.

King: Well, sir.

Bradshaw: If this must be reinforced, or anything of this nature, your answer must be the same, and they will proceed to sentence if you have nothing more to say.

King: I have nothing more to say. But I shall desire that this may be entered what I have said.

Bradshaw: The court then, sir, hath something to say unto you, which although I know it will be very unacceptable, yet notwithstanding they are willing and are resolved to discharge their duty.

Then Bradshaw went on in a long harangue endeavoring to justify their proceedings, misapplying law and history, and raking up and wresting whatsoever he thought fit for his purpose, alleging the examples of former treasons and rebellions, both at home and abroad, as authentic proofs, and concluding that the King was a tyrant, traitor, murderer, and public enemy to the Commonwealth of England.

His Majesty having with his wonted patience heard all these reproaches, answered: I would desire only one word before you give sentence, and that is that you would hear me concerning those great imputations that you have laid to my charge.

Bradshaw: Sir, you must give me now leave to go on, for I am not far from your sentence and your time is now past—

King: But I shall desire you will hear me a few words to you, for truly, whatever sentence you will put upon me in respect of those heavy imputations that I see by your speech you have put upon me, sir, it is very true that—

Bradshaw: Sir, I must put you in mind. Truly, sir, I would not willingly—at this time especially—interrupt you in anything you have to say that is proper for us to admit of. But, sir, you have not owned us as a court and you look upon us as a sort of people met together. And we know what language we receive from your party.

King: I know nothing of that.

Bradshaw: You disavow us as a court, and therefore for you to address yourself to us, [and] not to acknowledge us as a court to judge of what you say, it is not to be permitted. And the truth is, all along from the first time you were pleased to disavow and disown us, the court needed not to have heard you one word. For unless they be acknowledged a court and engaged, it is not proper for you to speak. Sir, we have given you too much liberty already and admitted of too much delay, and we may not admit of any further. Were it proper for us to do, we should hear you freely, and we should not have declined to have heard you at large what you could have said or proved on your behalf, whether for totally excusing or for in part excusing those great and heinous charges that in whole or in part are laid upon you. But, sir, I shall trouble you no longer. Your sins are of so large a dimension that—if you do but seriously think of them—they will drive you to a sad consideration, and they may improve in you a sad and serious repentance. And that the court doth heartily wish, that you may be so penitent for what you have done amiss, that God may have mercy at leastwise upon your better part. Truly, sir, for the other, it is our parts and duties to do that that the law prescribes. We are not here to create the law, but [merely] to say what it is. We cannot be unmindful of what the Scripture tells us, for to acquit the guilty is of equal abomination as to condemn the innocent [Prov. 17:15]. We may not acquit the guilty. What sentence the law affirms to a traitor, tyrant, a murderer, and a public enemy to the country, that sentence you are now to hear read unto you, and that is the sentence of the court. Make an oyez and command silence while the sentence is read.

Which done, their Clerk, Broughton, read the sentence drawn up in parchment. Which being read, Bradshaw added: "The sentence now read and published is the act, sentence, judgment, and resolution of the whole court." To which they all expressed their assent by standing up, as was before agreed and ordered.

His Majesty then said: Will you hear me a word, sir?

Bradshaw: Sir, you are not to be heard after the sentence.

King: No, sir?

Bradshaw: No, sir. By your favor, sir. Guard, withdraw your prisoner.

King: I may speak after sentence, by your favor, sir, I may speak after sentence, ever. By your favor, hold—the sentence, sir—I say, sir, I do—I am not suffered to speak, expect what justice other people will have.

His Majesty being taken away by the Guard, as he passed down the stairs the insolent soldiers scoffed at him, casting the smoke of their tobacco (a thing very distasteful unto him) in his face and throwing their pipes in his way. And one more insolent than the rest spitting in his face, His Majesty according to his wonted heroic patience took no more notice of so strange and barbarous an indignity than to wipe it off with his handkerchief.

As he passed along, hearing the rabble of soldiers crying out "Justice! Justice!" he said, "Poor souls, for a piece of money they would do so for their commanders."

Being brought first to Sir Robert Cotton's and thence to Whitehall, the soldiers continued their brutish carriage toward him, abusing all that seemed to show any respect or even pity to him, not suffering him to rest in his chamber, but thrusting in and smoking their tobacco and disturbing his privacy. But through all these trials (unusual to princes) he passed with such a calm and even temper that he let fall nothing unbeseeming his former majesty and magnanimity.

The Lord President's Speech

Citing historical precedents and quoting loosely from Scripture, Cicero, and such legal authorities as Bracton, Fortescue, and Coke, Bradshaw justifies the people's right to bring a tyrant to justice—Bradshaw's speech, alluded to in the two preceding documents, is given here in full

Lord President: The court then, sir, hath something else to say unto you, which, although I know it will be very unacceptable, yet notwithstanding they are willing and are resolved to discharge their duty.

Sir, you spake very well of a precious thing that you call peace, and it had been much to be wished that God had put it into your heart that you had as effectually and really endeavored and studied the peace of the kingdom as now in words you seem to pretend. But, as you were told the other day, actions must expound intentions; your actions have been clean contrary. And truly, sir, it doth appear plainly enough to them [i.e., to the court] that you have gone upon very erroneous principles. The kingdom hath felt it to their smart, and it will be no ease to you to think of it. For, sir, you have held yourself and let fall such language as if you had been no ways subject to the law, or that the law had not been your superior. Sir, the court is very well sensible of it—and I hope so are all the understanding people of England—that the law is your superior, that you ought to have ruled according to the law—you ought to have done so. Sir, I know very well your pretense hath been that you have done so. But, sir, the difference hath been: who shall be the expositors of this law, sir? Whether you and your party, out of courts of justice, shall take upon them to expound the law, or the courts of justice who are the expounders—nay, the sovereign and highest court of justice, the Parliament of England, that is not only the highest expounder but the sole maker of the law. Sir, for you to set yourself with your single judgment, and those that adhere unto you to set themselves against the resolution of the highest court of justice—that is not law. Sir, as the law is your superior, so truly, sir, there is something that is superior to the law and that is indeed the parent or author of the law—and that is the people of England. For, sir, as they are those that at the first (as other countries have done) did choose to themselves this form of government, even for justice's sake, that justice might be administered, that peace might be preserved, so, sir, they gave laws to their governors, according to which they should govern. And if those laws should have proved inconvenient or prejudicial to the public, they [i.e., the public] had a power in them, a power reserved and innate to alter them as they should see cause. Sir, it is very true what some of your side have said, "the King hath no equal within his realm" [Bracton, De legibus]. This court will say the same (while King) that you have not your peer in some sense, for you are "the greater among individuals." But they will aver again that you are "the lesser within the whole." And the same author [i.e., Bracton] tells you that "in the performance of justice" here you have no peer, but that "in receiving justice" you are "as if the last." This we know to be law—"the King hath a superior in God and the law, also in his court, barons, etc.," and so saith the same author. And truly, sir, he makes bold to go a little further—"they ought to bridle him." And, sir, we know very well the stories of old, those wars that were called the Barons' Wars, when the nobility of the land did stand up for the liberty and property of the subject and would not suffer the kings that did invade to play the tyrants freely, but called them to account for it. We know the truth, that they did "bridle" them. But, sir, if they [i.e., the nobility] do forbear to do their duty now and are not so mindful of their own honor and the kingdom's good as the barons of England of old were, certainly the Commons of England will not be unmindful of what is for their preservation and for their safety. "For the sake of enjoying justice, kings were appointed in olden time who were of virtuous character" [paraphrasing Cicero, De officiis, bk. 2, chap. 12]—this we learn, the end of having kings or any other governors is for the enjoying of justice, that's the end.

Now, sir, if so be the King will go contrary to that end, or any other governor will go contrary to the end of his government, sir, he must understand that he is but an officer in trust and he ought to discharge that trust, and they [i.e., the people] are to take order for the animadversion and punishment of such an offending governor. This is not the law of yesterday, sir—since the time of the division betwixt you and your people—but it is law of old. And we know very well the authors and authorities that do tell us what the law was in that point upon the election of kings, upon the oath that they took unto their people. And if they did not observe it, there were those things called Parliaments. The Parliaments were they that were to adjudge the plaints and wrongs done of the King and the Queen or their children, such wrongs especially when the people could have nowhere else any remedy. Sir, that hath been the people of England's case; they could not have their remedy elsewhere but in Parliament.

Sir, Parliaments were ordained for that purpose, to redress the grievances of the people. That was their main end. And truly, sir, if so be that the Kings of England had been rightly mindful of themselves, they were never more in majesty and state than in the Parliament [echoing Henry VIII in Ferrers' case]. But how forgetful some have been, stories have told us. We have a miserable, a lamentable, a sad experience of it throughout all England. I speak these things the rather to you because you were pleased to let fall the other day you thought you had as much knowledge in the law as most gentlemen in England. It is very well, sir, and truly, sir, it is very fit for the gentlemen of England to understand that law under which they must live and by which they must be governed. And then, sir, the Scripture says, "They that know their Master's will and do it not" [paraphrasing Luke 12:47]. What follows? The law is your master, the Acts of Parliament.

The Parliaments were to be kept anciently, we find in our old authors, twice in the year, that the subject upon any occasion might have a ready remedy and redress for his grievance. Afterwards, by several acts of Parliament in the days of your predecessor Edward III, they could be had but once a year. Sir, what the intermission of Parliaments hath been in your time, it is very well known, and the sad consequences of it. And what in the interim instead of these Parliaments hath been by you by an high and arbitrary hand introduced upon the people, that likewise hath been too well known and felt. But when God by His Providence had so far brought it about that you could no longer decline the calling of a Parliament, sir, yet it will appear what your ends were against your ancient and native Kingdom of Scotland. The Parliament of England not serving your ends against them, you were pleased to dissolve it [i.e., the Short Parliament, April–May 1640]. Another great necessity occasioned the calling of this Parliament [i.e., the Long Parliament], and what your designs and plots and endeavors all along have been for the crushing and confounding of this Parliament hath been very notorious to the whole kingdom. And truly, sir, in that you did strike at all—that had been a sure way to have brought about that that this charge lays upon you, your intention to subvert the fundamental laws of the land. For the great bulwark of the liberties of the people is the Parliament of England. And to subvert and root up that—which your aim hath been to do—certainly at one blow you had confounded the liberties and the property of England.

Truly, sir, it makes me call to mind—I cannot forbear to express it, for, sir, we must deal plainly with you, according to the merits of your cause, so is our commission—it makes me call to mind, these proceedings of yours, that [that] we read of a great Roman Emperor—by the way let us call him a great Roman Tyrant—Caligula, that wished that the people of Rome had had but one neck, that at one blow he might cut it off. And your proceedings hath been somewhat like to this. For the body of the people of England hath been—and where else?—represented but in the Parliament, and could you but have confounded that, you had at one blow cut off the neck of England. But God hath reserved better things for us and hath [been] pleased for to confound your designs and to break your forces and to bring your person into custody, that you might be responsible to justice.

Sir, we know very well that it is a question on your side very much pressed, by what precedent we shall proceed. Truly, sir, for precedent I shall not upon these occasions institute any long discourse, but it is no new thing to cite precedents almost of all nations where the people—when power hath been in their hands—have been made bold to call their kings to account, and where the change of government hath been upon occasion of the tyranny and misgovernment of those that have been placed over them. I will not spend time to mention France or Spain or the Empire or other countries—volumes may be written of it. But truly, sir, that of the Kingdom of Aragon, I shall think some of us have thought upon it, where they have the Justice of Aragon, that is a man as though placed in the middle betwixt the King of Spain and the people of the country, that if wrong be done by the King—he that is the King of Aragon—the Justice hath power to reform the wrong. And he is acknowledged to be the King's superior and is the grand preserver of their privileges and hath prosecuted Kings upon their miscarriages.

Sir, what the Tribunes of Rome were heretofore to the Roman Commonwealth and what the Ephori were to the Lacedaemonian state, we know that is the Parliament of England to the English state. And though Rome seemed to lose its liberty when once the emperors were, yet you shall find some famous acts of justice even done by the Senate of Rome—that great tyrant of his time, Nero, condemned and judged by the Senate. But truly, sir, to you I should not mention these foreign examples and stories. If you look but over [the River] Tweed, we find enough in your native Kingdom of Scotland. If we look to your first King Fergusius that your stories make mention of [i.e., the mythical Fergus I], he was an elective king. He died and left two sons, both in their minority. The kingdom made choice of their uncle, his brother, to govern in the minority. Afterwards, the elder brother giving small hopes to the people that he would rule or govern well, seeking to supplant that good uncle of his that governed them justly, they [i.e., the Scots] set the elder aside and took to the younger. Sir, if I should come to what your stories make mention of, you know very well you are the one-hundred-and-ninth King of Scotland, for to mention so many kings as that kingdom (according to their power and privilege) have made bold to deal withal, some to banish, some to imprison, and some to put to death, it would be too long. And as one of your own authors says [Buchanan, in *Rerum Scoticarum Historia*], it would be too long to recite the manifold examples that your own stories make mention of. "Kings," say they—"we created lawful kings at first." "Laws"—"we imposed equal laws upon them and ourselves" [Buchanan, *De jure regni apud Scotos*]. And as they are chosen by the suffrages of the people at the first, so upon just occasion by the same suffrages they may be taken down again. And we will be bold to say that no kingdom hath yielded more plentiful experience than your native Kingdom of Scotland hath done concerning the deposition and the punishment of their offending and transgressing kings. It is not far to go for an example near you—your grandmother [Mary, Queen of Scots] set aside and your father [James VI] an infant crowned.

And the state did it here in England. Here hath not been a want of some examples. They have made bold—the Parliament and the people of England—to call their kings to account. There are frequent examples of it in the Saxons' time, the time before the Conquest. Since the Conquest, there want not some precedents either. King Edward II [and] King Richard II were dealt with so by the Parliament, as they were deposed and deprived. And truly, sir, whoever shall look into their stories, they shall not find the articles that are charged upon them to come near to that height and capitalness of crimes that are laid to your charge, nothing near.

Sir, you were pleased to say the other day where you are in descent [i.e., inheritance], and I did not contradict it. But take it altogether, sir: you were as the charge speaks and not otherwise admitted King of England. But for that, you were pleased then to allege how that almost for a thousand years these things have been. Stories will tell you otherwise if you go higher than the time of the Conquest. [And] if you come down since the Conquest, you are the twenty-fourth King from William, called the Conqueror; you shall find more than one half of them to come merely from the state and not merely upon the point of descent. It were easy to be instanced to you, but the time must not be lost in that way. And truly, sir, what a grave and learned judge in his time, and well known to you, once said and hath left it for posterity, [is] that although there was such a thing as a descent many times, yet the Kings of England ever held the greatest assurance of their titles when they were declared by Parliament [Fortescue, "House of York"]. And, sir, your oath, the manner of your coronation doth show plainly that the Kings of England—although it's true by the law the next person in blood is designed—yet if there were just cause to refuse him, the people of England might do it. For there is a contract and bargain made between the King and his people, and your oath is taken. And certainly, sir, the bond is reciprocal, for as you are their liege lord, so they are your liege subjects. And we know very well—that hath been so much spoken of—"the bonding is two-fold and contains two ties" [paraphrasing Coke, in *Calvin's Case*]. This we know now—the one tie, the one bond, is the bond of protection that is due from the sovereign; the other is the bond of subjection that is due from the subject. Sir, if this bond be once broken, farewell sovereignty—"protection entails subjection, subjection entails protection" [Coke, in *Calvin's Case*].

These things may not be denied, sir. I speak it the rather—and I pray God it may work upon your heart—that you may be sensible of your miscarriages. For whether you have been (as by your office you ought to be) a Protector of England or the Destroyer of England, let all England judge, or all the world that hath looked upon it. Sir, though you have it by inheritance in the way that is spoken of, yet it must not be denied that your office was an office of trust, and indeed an office of the highest trust lodged in any single person, for as you were the grand administrator of justice and others were as your delegates to see it done throughout your realms. If your great office were to do justice and preserve your people from wrong and instead of doing that you will be the great wrongdoer yourself; if instead of being a conservator of the peace you will be the grand disturber of the peace—surely this is contrary to your office, contrary to your trust. Now, sir, if it be an office of inheritance—as you speak of your title by descent—let all men know that great offices are seizable and forfeitable, as if you had it but for a year or for your life. Therefore, sir, it will concern you to take into your serious consideration your great miscarriages in this kind. Truly, sir, I shall not particularize the many miscarriages of your reign whatsoever; they are famously known. It had been happy for the kingdom and happy for you too, if it had not been so much known, and so much felt, as the story of your miscarriages must needs be and hath been already.

Sir, that that we are now upon by the command of the highest court hath been and is to try and judge you for these great offenses of yours. Sir, the charge hath called you tyrant, a traitor, a murderer, and a public enemy to the Commonwealth of England. Sir, it had been well if that any of these terms might rightly and justly have been spared—if any one of them at all.

King: Ha!

Lord President: Truly, sir, we have been told, "he is a king as long as he rules well, but a tyrant when he violently oppresses the people entrusted to his care" [Bracton, *De legibus*]—and if that be the definition of a tyrant, then see how you come short of it in your actions, whether the highest tyrant by that way of arbitrary government and that you have sought for to introduce and that you have sought to put—you were putting—upon the people, whether that was not as high an act of tyranny as any of your predecessors were guilty of—nay, many degrees beyond it.

Sir, the term traitor cannot be spared. We shall easily agree it must denote and suppose a breach of trust, and it must suppose it to be done by a superior. And therefore, sir, as the people of England might have incurred that respecting you, if they had been truly guilty of it as to the definition of law, so on the other side when you did break your trust to the kingdom, you did break your trust to your superior. For the kingdom is that for which you were trusted. And, therefore, sir, for this breach of trust when you are called to account, you are called to account by your superiors—"when a king is summoned to judgment by the people, the lesser is summoned by the greater." And, sir, the people of England cannot be so far wanting to themselves, God having dealt so miraculously and gloriously for them, they having power in their hands and their great enemy, they must proceed to do justice to themselves and to you. For, sir, the court could heartily desire that you would lay your hand upon your heart and consider what you have done amiss, that you would endeavor to make your peace with God.

Truly, sir, these are your high crimes—tyranny and treason. And there is a third thing too, if those had not been, and that is murder, which is laid to your charge. All the bloody murders that have been committed since this time that the division was betwixt you and your people must be laid to your charge that have been acted or committed in these late wars. Sir, it is an heinous and crying sin, and truly, sir, if any man will ask us what punishment is due to a murderer, let God's law, let man's law, speak. Sir, I will presume that you are so well read in Scripture as to know what God Himself hath said concerning the shedding of man's blood. Genesis 9 [and] Numbers 35 will tell you what the punishment is of that innocent blood that has been shed, whereby indeed the land still stands defiled with that blood, and as the text hath it, it can no way be cleansed but with the shedding of the blood of him that shed this blood [Num. 35:33]. Sir, we know no dispensation from this blood in that commandment, "Thou shalt do no murder" [Matt. 19:18]. We do not know but that it extends to kings as well as to the meanest peasants, the meanest of the people—the command is universal. Sir, God's law forbids it, man's law forbids [it], nor do we know that there is any manner of exception—not even in man's laws—for the punishment of murder in you. 'Tis true that in the case of kings, every private hand was not to put forth itself to this work for their reformation and punishment. But, sir, the people represented, having power in their hands—had there been but one willful act of murder by you committed—had power to have convened you and to have punished you for it.

But then, sir, the weight that lies upon you in all those respects that have been spoken, by reason of your tyranny, treason, breach of trust, and the murders that have been committed, surely, sir, it must drive you into a sad consideration concerning your eternal condition. As I said at first, I know it cannot be pleasing to you to hear any such things as these [that] are mentioned unto you from this court—for so we do call ourselves and justify ourselves to be a court, and a High Court of Justice, authorized by the highest and solemnest court of the kingdom, as we have often said. And although you do yet endeavor what you may to dis-court us, yet we do take knowledge of ourselves to be such a court as can administer justice to you and we are bound, sir, in duty to do it. Sir, all I shall say before the reading of your sentence it is but this—the court does heartily desire that you will seriously think of those evils that you stand guilty of. Sir, you said well to us the other day, you wished us to have God before our eyes. Truly, sir, I hope all of us have so. That God that we know is a King of Kings and Lord of Lords, that God with whom there is no respect of persons, that God that is the avenger of innocent blood—we have that God before us, that God that does bestow a curse upon them that withhold their hands from shedding of blood, which is in the case of guilty malefactors and those that do deserve death. That God we have before our eyes, and were it not that the conscience of our duty hath called us unto this place and this employment, sir, you should have had no appearance of a court here. But, sir, we must prefer the discharge of our duty unto God and unto the kingdom before any other respect whatsoever. And although at this time many of us—if not all of us—are severely threatened by some of your party, what[ever] they intend to do, sir, we do here declare that we shall not decline or forbear the doing of our duty in the administration of justice even to you, according to the merit of your offense, although God should permit those men to effect all that bloody design in hand against us. Sir, we will say and we will declare it as those children in the Fiery Furnace that would not worship the golden image that Nebuchadnezzar had set up, that their God was able to deliver them from that danger that they were near unto, but yet if He would not do it, yet notwithstanding that, they would not fall down and worship the image [referring to Dan. 3:17–18]. We shall thus apply it, that though we should not be delivered from those bloody hands and hearts that conspire the overthrow of the kingdom in general—of us in particular—for acting in this great work of justice, though we should perish in the work, yet by God's grace and by God's strength we will go on with it. And this is all our resolutions.

Sir, I say for yourself we do heartily wish and desire that God would be pleased to give you a sense of your sins, that you would see wherein you have done amiss, that you may cry unto Him that God would deliver you from bloodguiltiness. A good king [i.e., David] was once guilty of that particular thing and was clear otherwise, saving in the matter of Uriah. Truly, sir, the story tells us that he was a repentant king, and it signifies enough that he had died for it, but that God was pleased to accept of him and to give him his pardon: "Thou shalt not die, but the child shall die for as much as thou hast given cause to the enemies of God to blaspheme" [paraphrasing 2 Sam. 12:13–14]. I shall not trouble you further, I shall—

King: I would desire only one word before you give sentence, and that is that you would hear me concerning those great imputations that you have laid to my charge.

House of Commons

Proclamation of the King's successor to be prohibited

The House considered, in case of execution of the King, that if any in the kingdom should attempt or go about to proclaim Prince

Charles or any of that line King of England, as usually hath been done in this nation after the death of Kings, and the better to leave all without excuse herein, they ordered that a committee should be appointed to draw a proclamation to be published throughout the kingdom to declare it High Treason in any person or persons to proclaim any King of England without the consent of the Parliament, and that none under pain of imprisonment or such other punishments as shall be thought fit to be inflicted on them shall preach or speak anything contrary to the present proceedings of the supreme authority of this nation, the Commons of England assembled in Parliament.

The House agrees to the King's last wishes

A member of the Army acquainted some Members of Parliament with the desires of His Majesty that, in respect sentence of death was passed upon him and the time of his execution might be nigh, the House would give him leave to see his children, and also that he might have the benefit to receive the Sacrament and prepare himself for death, and in order thereunto that he might have Dr. Juxon, late Bishop of London, to have the privilege to be private with him in his chamber. The House ordered the same accordingly.

The House ordered that their members should be required to meet on Monday morning at the House by 8 of the clock, there being much business that would be offered to the House on that day.

Other News

Devotions

This night the King lodged in Whitehall. Sunday, Dr. Juxon preached before the King in his private lodgings. The High Court, and the Lord President with them, kept a Fast in the Chapel at Whitehall on Sunday.

Monday, 29 January 1649

House of Commons

The House reaffirms the exclusion of the purged members

This day the House sat early (as was appointed) and one of the late secluded members coming into the House occasioned them to consider of that business. Upon which they voted that such members as voted 5 December last that the King's concessions were a ground of settling a peace in this nation should not be readmitted but disabled to sit any longer members for the future.

The Dutch intercede to save the King

The Dutch Ambassadors had their audience in the House. They read their Instructions and Letters of Credence in French but had no copies thereof in English (as usual), but [they] said copies should be prepared against tomorrow morning. Their desire was to intercede for the King's life and to keep and preserve a fair correspondency between this nation and the States of Holland. But having no transcripts ready and being unwilling to leave the original, the House at that time could not proceed in debate thereof.

Act passed for altering judicial proceedings

This day an act passed for alteration of several names and forms heretofore used in courts, writs, grants, patents, etc., and settling of proceedings in courts of law, justice, and equity, within the Kingdoms of England and Ireland, Dominion of Wales, and Town of Berwick-upon-Tweed, as followeth:

> Be it enacted by this present Parliament and by authority of the same, that in all courts of law, justice, or equity; and in all writs, grants, patents, commissions, indictments, informations, suits, returns of writs; and in all fines, recoveries, exemplifications, recognizances, process and proceedings of law, justice, or equity within the Kingdoms of England and Ireland, Dominion of Wales, and Town of Berwick-upon-

Tweed, instead of the name, style, title, and attestation of the
King heretofore used, that from henceforth the name, style,
title, and attestation of "Guardians of the Liberty of England
by the Authority of Parliament" shall be used, and no other.
And the date shall be the year of our Lord, and none other.
And that all duties, profits, penalties, issues, fines, amerce-
ments, and forfeitures whatsoever which heretofore were
sued for in the name of the King shall from henceforth be
prosecuted, sued for and recovered in the said name of
Guardians of the Liberty of England by the Authority of
Parliament, and no other. And in all or any of the proceedings aforesaid, where the words were "Jurors for the King,"
from henceforth it shall be "Jurors for the Commonwealth."
And where the words in any of the proceedings aforesaid
used to be "Against the Peace, our Authority, or our Crown,"
that from henceforth these words "Against the Public Peace"
instead of them or any of them shall be only used. And all
judges, justices, officers and ministers of justice whatsoever
are to take notice hereof, and are hereby authorized and
required to proceed accordingly and not otherwise. And
whatsoever henceforth shall be done contrary to this act shall
be, and is hereby declared to be, null and void, provided
always that all writs issued out of the Chancery, and all writs
and patents of the Justices of the one bench and of the other,
Barons of the Exchequer, commissioners of oyer and termin-
er, jail delivery, and justices of the peace, and all other commissions, patents, and grants, made and passed under the
Great Seal of England shall stand good and effectual in the
law notwithstanding the death of the King, anything in this
act or in any article therein contained, or any law, statute, or
custom to the contrary thereof in any wise notwithstanding.
And it is hereby further ordained and enacted by the authority aforesaid that all writs original already issued out under
the Great Seal, and all actions, suits, bills, or plaints now
depending in any court of record in Westminster Hall or any
other court of record, and all process, pleas, demurs, continu-
ances, and proceedings in every such action, actions, suits,
bills, and plaints, shall be returnable, stand good and effectual, and be prosecuted and sued forth in such manner and

form, and in the same state, condition, and order; the said changes and alterations to be as before in this act is expressed, the death of the King, or any law, custom, or usage to the contrary thereof in any wise notwithstanding. And that any variance that shall be occasioned by reason thereof touching any the said writs, process, or proceedings in the name, style, attestation, or otherwise, shall not be in any wise material as concerning any default or error to be alleged or objected thereunto.

The King Prepares for Death

Devotions and farewells

The King was Saturday and Sunday at Whitehall. Dr. Juxon sat up with him all Saturday night. Sunday he dined and supped in his bedchamber and seemed very cheerful. This day means was made to deliver a letter to him from the Prince, which the King no sooner received but burned it.

This day the King was removed to St. James's, where his children from Syon House came to visit him but stayed not long. He took the Princess in his arms and kissed her, gave her his blessing and two seals that he had wherein were two diamonds; she wept bitterly. The Prince Elector, [the] Duke of Richmond, and others made suit to see him, which he refused. This night he lay at St. James's.

The King's Farewell to his Children

A fuller account of the King's last meeting with his daughter Elizabeth (aged 13) and his son Henry (aged 8)

His children being come to meet him, he first gave his blessing to the Lady Elizabeth and bade her remember to tell her brother James, whenever she should see him, that it was his father's last desire that he should no more look upon [Prince] Charles as his eldest brother only but be obedient unto him as his sovereign, and that they should love one another and forgive their father's enemies. Then said the King to her, "Sweetheart, you will forget this." "No," said she, "I shall

Three Children of Charles I: Three of Charles's children fell into the hands of Parliament during the Civil War. They are portrayed here in a charming miniature painted about a year before the trial. James, Duke of York, is in the middle, flanked by the Princess Elizabeth and Henry, Duke of Gloucester. Before the trial, James managed to escape to join his mother in France, but his brother and sister remained in custody and were allowed to visit their father the day before his execution. At their emotional last meeting, Charles cut through the tears to insist that they now honor their eldest brother, Charles—then at The Hague—as their sovereign. Rumor had it that Parliamentary moderates intended to crown the eight-year-old Henry as their puppet, and this concerned Charles deeply. Elizabeth died the next year, still a prisoner; Henry succumbed to smallpox just after the Restoration; and James succeeded in 1685 only to be deposed in the Glorious Revolution of 1688. Miniature by John Hoskins, ca. early 1648. Fitzwilliam Museum, Cambridge. Reproduced by kind permission.

never forget it whilst I live," and pouring forth abundance of tears, promised him to write down the particulars.

Then the King taking the Duke of Gloucester upon his knee, said "Sweetheart, now they will cut off thy father's head," upon which words, the child looked very steadfastly upon him. "Mark, child, what I say. They will cut off my head, and perhaps make thee a king. But mark what I say, you must not be a king so long as your brothers

Charles and James do live, for they will cut off your brothers' heads (when they can catch them) and cut off thy head too at last. And therefore I charge you, do not be made a king by them."

At which, the child, sighing, said, "I will be torn in pieces first." Which falling so unexpectedly from one so young, it made the King rejoice exceedingly.

High Court of Justice

Preparations for the King's Execution—meeting in the Painted Chamber, forty-eight commissioners present, as reported in Phelps's Journal

Upon report made from the committee for considering the time and place of the executing of the judgment against the King, that the said committee have resolved that the open street before Whitehall is a fit place, and that the said committee conceive it fit that the King be there executed the morrow, the King having already notice thereof. The court approved thereof, and ordered a warrant to be drawn for that purpose, which said warrant was accordingly drawn and agreed unto, and ordered to be engrossed, which was done and signed and sealed accordingly as followeth:

The Death Warrant: Time has faded the signatures, but the fifty-nine seals still stand out clearly on the warrant ordering the King's execution "by the severing of his head from his body." Issuing the warrant evidently took more effort than the official trial record reveals. Although the warrant is dated 29 January, a quarter of the signatures belong to judges who were absent that day, whereas several of the judges known to be present in court did not sign. Furthermore, close inspection of the original shows that the dates of the King's sentencing and death were added over erasures. Finding officers willing to execute the judges' order certainly proved difficult, given the fact that the names of two of the addressees, Colonels Hacker and Phayre, also were written over prior erasures. By the time of the Restoration, eighteen signers had died and fifteen had managed to escape the country, but the remaining twenty-six were put on trial. A handful of the lucky or well-connected were pardoned, including John Downes, whose whispered doubts about the sentencing made up for the fact that he then allowed Cromwell to browbeat him into signing the warrant. Many received life sentences, and nine were executed. The fact that Bradshaw, Cromwell, and Ireton were already dead did not spare them: twelve years to the day after the King's execution, their exhumed corpses were hung on a gibbet and beheaded. Their heads were displayed atop Westminster Hall for many years. From the House of Lords Record Office. Reproduced by permission of the Clerk of the Records.

At the High Court of Justice for the trying and judging of Charles Stuart, King of England, January 29, 1649.

Whereas Charles Stuart, King of England, is and standeth convicted, attainted, and condemned of High Treason and other high crimes, and sentence upon Saturday last was pronounced against him by this court to be put to death by the severing of his head from his body, of which sentence execution yet remaineth to be done, these are therefore to will and require you to see the said sentence executed in the open street before Whitehall, upon the morrow, being the thirtieth day of this instant month of January, between the hours of ten in the morning and five in the afternoon of the same day, with full effect. And for so doing, this shall be your sufficient warrant. And these are to require all officers, soldiers, and others, the good people of this nation of England, to be assisting unto you in this service.

Given under our hands and seals.

Sealed and subscribed by: John Bradshaw, Thomas Grey, Oliver Cromwell, Edward Whalley, Michael Livesey, John Okey, John Danvers, John Bourchier, Henry Ireton, Thomas Mauleverer, John Blakiston, John Hutchinson, William Goffe, Thomas Pride, Peter Temple, Thomas Harrison, John Hewson, Henry Smith, Peregrine Pelham, Simon Mayne, Thomas Horton, John Jones, John Moore, Hardress Waller, Gilbert Millington, George Fleetwood, John Alured, Robert Lilburne, William Say, Anthony Stapley, Richard Deane, Robert Tichborne, Humphrey Edwards, Daniel Blagrave, Owen Rowe, William Purefoy, Adrian Scrope, James Temple, Augustine Garland, Edmund Ludlow, Henry Marten, Vincent Potter, William Constable, Richard Ingoldsby, William Cawley, John Barkstead, Isaac Ewer, John Dixwell, Valentine Walton, Gregory Norton, Thomas Chaloner, Thomas Wogan, John Venn, Gregory Clement, John Downes, Thomas Waite, Thomas Scot, John Carew, Miles Corbet.

To Colonel Francis Hacker, Colonel Huncks, and Lieutenant Colonel Phayre, and to every of them.

It was ordered that the Officers of the Ordnance within the Tower of London or any other officer or officers of the store within the said

Tower in whose hands or custody the bright Execution Ax for the executing [of] malefactors is, do forthwith deliver unto Edward Dendy, Esq., Sergeant at Arms attending this court, or his deputy or deputies, the said Ax. And for their or either of their so doing, this shall be their warrant.

The court adjourned till tomorrow morning at 9 of the clock.

Other News

The Scots object to the King's condemnation

From Scotland they write that the ministers of the Kirk preach against the Army in England and their proceedings against their King. They say they are bound by their Covenant to preserve monarchy, and that in the race [i.e., bloodline] of the present King.

Naval skirmishes—news from Dartmouth

We had the other day a fight of Prince Rupert, with about fourteen revolting ships sailing by our coast and bending towards Ireland. They drive the whole Channel before them and seize upon many several vessels, but [only] one of great value laden with cloth worth £5,000. We apprehended a great neglect in not having any Navy abroad. One of this fleet was driven in here the twenty-sixth, where she now remains. The master reports that the fleet is very poorly victualed and worse manned, having got but four hundred mariners amongst them.

Tuesday, 30 January 1649

House of Commons

An Act Prohibiting the Proclaiming Any Person to be King of England or Ireland or the Dominions thereof—reported out of committee and read twice in the morning session, the act is given its third reading and passed in the afternoon

Whereas Charles Stuart, King of England, being for the notorious treasons, tyrannies, and murders committed by him in the late unnatural and cruel wars condemned to death, whereupon after execution of the same several pretenses may be made and title set on foot unto the kingly office to the apparent hazard of the public peace, for prevention thereof be it enacted and ordained by this present Parliament, and by authority of the same, that no person or persons whatsoever do presume to proclaim, declare, publish, or any way promote Charles Stuart, son of the said Charles, commonly called the Prince of Wales, or any other person, to be King or Chief Magistrate of England or of Ireland, or of any the dominions belonging to them or either of them, by color of inheritance, succession, election, or any other claim whatsoever, without the free consent of the people in Parliament first had and signified by a particular act or ordinance for that purpose, any statute, law, usage, or custom to the contrary hereof in any wise notwithstanding.

And be it further enacted and ordained, and it is hereby enacted and ordained, that whosoever shall contrary to this act proclaim, declare, publish, or any way promote the said Charles Stuart (the son) or any other person to be King or Chief Magistrate of England or of Ireland, or of any the dominions belonging to them or to either of them, without the said consent in Parliament signified as aforesaid, shall be deemed and adjudged a traitor to the Commonwealth and shall suffer pains of death and such other punishments as belong to the crime of High Treason. And all officers, as well civil as military, and all other well-affected persons are hereby authorized and required forthwith to apprehend all such offenders and to bring them in safe custody to the next justice of the peace, that they may be proceeded against accordingly.

The King's Execution

A contemporary published account of the King's Execution

About ten in the morning the King was brought from St. James's walking on foot through the Park, with a regiment of foot part before and part behind him, with colors flying, drums beating, his private guard of partizans with some of his gentlemen before and some

The King on the Scaffold: Wearing his nightcap, Charles says some final words to Dr. Juxon. Troops on foot and horseback are in position to control the crowd. The headsman stands in readiness, disguised so successfully by a mask and wig that his identity remains unknown to this day. Once Charles knelt down to put his head on the block, the black cloth draped around the scaffold railings hid him from view. Fearing that he might struggle, Charles's executioners were prepared if necessary to tie him down to iron staples that they had driven into the scaffold floor for that purpose. Detail of an illustration from *The True Characters of, The Educations, Inclinations and Several Dispositions of those Bloody and Barbarous Persons who Sate as Judges* (London, 1660). By permission of the British Library.

behind bareheaded, Dr. Juxon next behind him, and Colonel Thomlinson (who had the charge of him) talking with the King bareheaded, from the Park up the stairs into the gallery [in Whitehall], and so into the cabinet chamber where he used to lie, where he continued at his devotion, refusing to dine (having before taken the Sacrament), only about an hour before he came forth he drank a glass of claret wine and ate a piece of bread about twelve at noon.

From thence he was accompanied by Dr. Juxon, Colonel Thomlinson, and other officers formerly appointed to attend him, and the private guard of partizans and musketeers on each side, through the Banqueting House, adjoining to which the Scaffold was erected between Whitehall Gate and the gate leading into the gallery from St. James's.

The Scaffold was hung round with black and the floor covered with black, and the Ax and Block laid in the middle of the Scaffold. There were divers companies of foot and troops of horse placed on the one side of the Scaffold towards King Street and on the other side towards Charing Cross, and the multitudes of people that came to be spectators [were] very great.

The King being come upon the Scaffold looked very earnestly on the Block and asked Colonel Hacker if there were no higher, and then spake thus, directing his speech chiefly to Colonel Thomlinson.

King: I shall be very little heard of anybody here, I shall therefore speak a word unto you here. Indeed I could hold my peace very well, if I did not think that holding my peace would make some men think that I did submit to the guilt as well as to the punishment. But I think it is my duty to God first, and to my country, for to clear myself both as an honest man, a good king, and a good Christian.

I shall begin first with my innocency. In truth, I think it not very needful for me to insist long upon this, for all the world knows that I never did begin a war with the two Houses of Parliament. And I call God to witness—to whom I must shortly make an account—that I never did intend for to encroach upon their privileges. They began upon me: it is the Militia they began upon. They confessed that the Militia was mine, but they thought it fit for to have it from me. And to be short, if anybody will look to the dates of commissions—of their commissions and mine—and likewise to the declarations, will see clearly that they began these unhappy troubles, not I. So that as [to] the guilt of these enormous crimes that are laid against me, I hope in God that God will clear me of it. I will not; I'm in charity. God forbid that I should lay it upon the two Houses of Parliament. There is no necessity of [doing so] either. I hope they are free of this guilt, for I do believe that ill instruments between them and me have been the chief cause of all this bloodshed, so that by way of speaking, as I find myself clear of this, I hope and pray God that they may too. Yet for all this, God forbid that I should be so ill a Christian as not to say that God's judgments are just upon me. Many times He does pay justice by an unjust sentence; that is ordinary. I will only say this, that an unjust sentence [i.e., the attainder in 1641 of Lord Strafford] that I suffered for to take effect, is punished now by an unjust sentence upon me. That is, so far I have said, to show you that I am an innocent man.

Now for to show you that I am a good Christian. I hope there is *(pointing to Dr. Juxon)* a good man that will bear me witness that I have forgiven all the world and even those in particular that have been the chief causers of my death. Who they are, God knows; I do not desire to know. I pray God forgive them. But this is not all—my charity must go further. I wish that they may repent, for indeed they have committed a great sin in that particular. I pray God with St. Stephen that this be not laid to their charge—nay not only so, but that they may take the right way to the peace of the kingdom, for my charity commands me not only to forgive particular men, but my charity commands me to endeavor to the last gasp the peace of the kingdom. So, sirs, I do wish with all my soul, and I do hope there is some here *(turning to some gentlemen that wrote)* will carry it further, that they may endeavor the peace of the kingdom.

Now, sirs, I must show you both how you are out of the way and [I] will put you in the way. First you are out of the way, for certainly all the way you ever have had yet—as I could find by anything—is in the way of conquest. Certainly this is an ill way. For conquest, sirs, in my opinion is never just, except there be a good just cause, either for matter of wrong or just title. And then if you go beyond it, the first quarrel that you have to it, that makes it unjust at the end that was just at first.

But if it be only matter of conquest, then it is a great robbery; as a pirate said to Alexander the Great that he was the great robber, he [the pirate] was but a petty robber. And so, sirs, I do think the way that you are in is much out of the way. Now, sirs, for to put you in the way. Believe it, you will never do right, nor God will never prosper you, until you give God His due, the King his due—that is, my successors—and the people their due. I am as much for them as any of you. You must give God His due by regulating rightly His Church (according to His Scripture) which is now out of order. For to set you in a way particularly, now I cannot; but only this: a national synod freely called, freely debating among themselves, must settle this, when that every opinion is freely and clearly heard. For the King, indeed I will not—(then turning to a gentleman that touched the Ax he said, "Hurt not the Ax that may hurt me," meaning if he did blunt the edge)—for the King, the laws of the land will clearly instruct you for that. Therefore, because it concerns my own particular, I only give you a touch of it. For the people—and truly I desire their liberty and freedom as much as anybody whomsoever—but I must tell you that their liberty and their freedom consists in having of government those laws by which their life and their goods may be most their own. It is not for having share in government, sirs; that is nothing pertaining to them. A subject and a sovereign are clean different things. And therefore until they do that—I mean, that you do put the people in that liberty as I say—certainly they will never enjoy themselves. Sirs, it was for this that now I am come here. If I would have given way to an arbitrary way for to have all laws changed according to the power of the sword, I needed not to have come here. And therefore I tell you—and I pray God it be not laid to your charge—that I am the martyr of the people.

In truth, sirs, I shall not hold you much longer, for I will only say this to you, that in truth I could have desired some little time longer because that I would have put this that I have said in a little more order and a little better digested than I have done. And therefore I hope you will excuse me. I have delivered my conscience. I pray God that you do take those courses that are best for the good of the kingdom and your own salvations.

Dr. Juxon: Will Your Majesty, though it may be very well known Your Majesty's affections to religion, yet it may be expected that you should say somewhat for the world's satisfaction.

King: I thank you very heartily, my lord, for that I had almost forgotten it. In truth, sirs, my conscience in religion, I think is very well known to all the world. And therefore I declare before you all that I die a Christian according to the profession of the Church of England as I found it left me by my father. And this honest man (*pointing to Dr. Juxon*) I think will witness it.

Then turning to the officers, the King said: Sirs, excuse me for this same. I have a good cause, and I have a gracious God. I will say no more.

Then turning to Colonel Hacker, he said: Take care they do not put me to pain. And, sir, this, and it please you—

But then a gentleman coming near the Ax, the King said: Take heed of the Ax, pray take heed of the Ax!

Then the King speaking to the Executioner said: I shall say but very short prayers, and when I thrust out my hands . . .

Then the King called to Dr. Juxon for his nightcap, and having put it on, he said to the Executioner, "Does my hair trouble you?" who desired him to put it all under his cap, which the King did accordingly by the help of the Executioner and the Bishop.

Then the King turning to Dr. Juxon said: I have a good cause, and a gracious God on my side.

Dr. Juxon: There is but one stage more. This stage is turbulent and troublesome. It is a short one. But you may consider it will soon carry you a very great way—it will carry you from Earth to Heaven, and there you shall find a great deal of cordial joy and comfort.

King: I go from a corruptible to an incorruptible crown, where no disturbance can be, no disturbance in the world.

Dr. Juxon: You are exchanged from a temporal to an eternal crown—a good exchange.

The King then said to the Executioner, "Is my hair well?" Then the King took off his cloak and his George [i.e., the Garter insignia],

giving his George to Dr. Juxon, saying, "Remember" (it is thought for to give it to the Prince). The King put off his doublet, and being in his waistcoat put his cloak on again, then looking upon the Block said to the Executioner, "You must set it fast."

Executioner: It is fast, sir.
King: It might have been a little higher.
Executioner: It can be no higher, sir.
King: When I put out my hands this way *(stretching them out)*— then . . .

After that, having said two or three words (as he stood) to himself with hands and eyes lifted up, immediately stooping down laid his neck upon the Block, and then the Executioner again putting his hair under his cap, the King said (thinking he had been going to strike), "Stay for the sign!"

Executioner: Yes I will, and it please Your Majesty.

And after a very little pause, the King stretching forth his hands, the Executioner at one blow severed his head from his body. Then when the King's head was cut off, the Executioner held it up and showed it to the spectators.

And his body was put in a coffin covered with black velvet for that purpose, and conveyed into his lodgings there. And from thence it was carried to his house at St. James's, where his body was put in a coffin of lead laid there to be seen by the people.

Epilogue

House of Lords and Monarchy Abolished

From the Journals of the House of Commons for 6 February 1649

Resolved, that the House of Peers in Parliament is useless and dangerous and ought to be abolished, and that an act be brought in to that purpose. [The resulting act was passed and ordered published on 19 March].

The Execution: The executioner has just struck and lifts Charles's head for the crowd to see. Dr. Juxon and Colonel Thomlinson hold various articles of the King's clothing while Colonel Hacker (furthest right on the scaffold) superintends the execution. So momentous a scene inspired many popular prints, all of them marred by various inaccuracies. The artist of this German version was probably working from secondhand descriptions of the event: the black-hung railings have been omitted, and in reality the block was only six or seven inches tall—a size more effective for purposes of decapitation, but one requiring the King to lie almost flat on his face. Detail of an anonymous contemporary German engraving. By courtesy of the Department of Western Art, Ashmolean Museum, Oxford.

From the Journals of the House of Commons for 7 February 1649

Resolved, that it hath been found by experience, and this House doth declare, that the office of a King in this nation, and to have the power thereof in any single person, is unnecessary, burdensome, and dangerous to the liberty, safety and public interest of the people of this nation, and therefore ought to be abolished, and that an act be brought in to that purpose. [The resulting act was passed and ordered published on 17 March].

The "Scaffold George": Stripped of its diamonds and now somewhat dented, this is the insignia of the Order of the Garter that Charles handed to Dr. Juxon just moments before his death, with a reminder that it be delivered to his heir, Prince Charles. The new regime, fearing so dangerous a gesture, had the George seized and auctioned off. Colonel Thomlinson had witnessed the King's request and must have been ashamed of his colleagues' disregard for their prisoner's last wish, for he seems to have purchased the George anonymously through a middleman and arranged for it to be delivered to the new King. At the Restoration he received a full pardon. From the Royal Collection, Windsor Castle: copyright reserved to Her Majesty Queen Elizabeth II. Reproduced by gracious permission of The Queen.

The King's Funeral

The aftermath of the Execution, as recalled by the royalist John Nalson

His blood was taken up by divers persons for different ends: by some as trophies of their villainy; by others as relics of a martyr, and in some hath had the same effect (by the blessing of God) which was often found in his Sacred Touch when living [i.e., the traditional miraculous healing power of the royal touch].

The malice of his enemies ended not with his life, for when his body was carried to St. James's to be opened, they directed their empirics [i.e., surgeons] to search for such symptoms as might disgrace his person or his posterity. But herein they were prevented by an honest intruder, who gave a true account of his sound and excellent temperament.

Being embalmed and laid in a coffin of lead to be seen for some days by the people, at length upon Wednesday the seventh of February it was delivered to four of his servants (Herbert, Mildmay, Preston, and Joiner) who with some others in mourning equipage attended the hearse [i.e., the bier] that night to Windsor, and placed it in the room which was formerly the King's bedchamber.

Next day it was removed into the Dean's Hall, which was hung with black and made dark, and lights were set burning round the hearse. About three after noon, the Duke of Richmond, the Marquis of Hertford, the Earls of Southampton and Lindsey, and the Bishop of London (others that were sent too refusing that last service to the best of princes) came thither with two votes passed that morning, whereby the ordering of the King's burial was committed to the Duke, provided that the expenses thereof exceeded not £500. This order they showed to Colonel Whichcot, the Governor of the Castle, desiring the interment might be in St. George's Chapel and according to the form of *The Book of Common Prayer.* The latter request the Governor denied, saying that it was improbable the Parliament would permit the use of what they had so solemnly abolished and therein destroy their own act. The lords replied that there was a difference betwixt destroying their own act and dispensing with it, and that no power so binds its own hands as to disable itself in some cases. But all prevailed not.

The Governor had caused an ordinary grave to be dug in the body of the church of Windsor for the interment of the corpse, which

the lords disdaining found means by the direction of an honest man (one of the old knights) to use an artifice to discover a vault in the middle of the choir by the hollow sound they might perceive in knocking with a staff upon that place, that so it might seem to be their own accidental finding out and no person receive blame for the discovery. This place they caused to be opened, and entering saw one large coffin of lead in the middle of the vault covered with a velvet pall and a lesser on one side (supposed to be Henry VIII and his beloved Queen Jane Seymour); on the other side was room left for another (probably intended for Queen Catherine Parr, who survived him) where they thought fit to lay the King.

Hither the hearse was borne by the officers of the garrison, the four lords bearing up the corners of the velvet pall, and the Bishop of London following. And in this manner was this great King, upon Friday, the ninth of February, about three after noon, silently and without other solemnity than of sighs and tears, committed to the earth, the velvet pall being thrown into the vault over the coffin, to which was fastened an inscription in lead of these words:

King Charles, 1649.

Sources

List of Sources

Agreement: *An Agreement Prepared for the People of England* (London, 1649). Endorsed by the General Council of the Army on 19 January 1649, presented to the House of Commons the next day, and published soon afterwards, the "Agreement of the People" encapsulates the political program of the Levellers, as moderated after lengthy negotiations with the officers on the General Council.

CJ: *Journals of the House of Commons.* Vol. 6 of the series records the actions of the House from September 1648 to August 1651.

Firth & Rait: C. H. Firth and R. S. Rait (eds.), *Acts and Ordinances of the Interregnum* (3 vols., London, 1911). A collection of Parliament's legislation during the period 1642–60.

KCT: *King Charls his Tryal at the High Court of Justice* (2d ed., London, 1650). This edition corrects and amplifies the first edition, published in February 1649, which itself was based on a series of pamphlets issued while the trial was in progress. It provides a transcript of the proceedings in open court as well as the text of the King's scaffold speech. Although its publication was officially licensed, *KCT* does not appear to be significantly biased against the King either in the way it reports the dialogue between the King

149

and the court or in the way it describes the reactions of spectators at the trial.

Muddiman: J. G. Muddiman, *Trial of King Charles the First* (Edinburgh, [1928]). An account of the trial based on the manuscript journal (which it transcribes) written by the two Clerks of the Court, Phelps and Broughton. There are indications that the record was prepared after the trial and that it is not as candid as either the Phelps Journal (included in Nalson) or the transcripts published in *KCT*. But because it benefited from contemporary editorial attention (presumably by Phelps and Broughton, if not by Bradshaw himself), Muddiman's source is helpful in establishing the text of Bradshaw's sentencing speech, whose frequent Latin quotations and obscure allusions are imperfectly captured in *KCT*.

Nalson: John Nalson, *A True Copy of the Journal of the High Court of Justice for the Tryal of K. Charles I* (London, 1684). Nalson transcribes the journal kept by John Phelps, one of the two Clerks of the Court, which was accepted as the official record of the trial by the House of Commons; it summarizes the actions of the court in its private as well as public sessions. Nalson also includes other contemporary documents (such as an account of the King's farewell to his children) and occasionally interjects his own personal (strongly royalist) commentary.

Rushworth: John Rushworth, *Historical Collections* (8 vols., London, 1721–22). Excerpts of news accounts and pamphlets compiled by John Rushworth, a lawyer and former government censor who at the time of the trial was secretary to Lord Fairfax, and was thus a close witness to the proceedings. Vol. 7 of his collection covers the period from early 1645 through the King's execution and draws heavily on the weekly newspaper *A Perfect Diurnall*.

Sources by Day

Prologue: Rushworth, VII, 1349, 1350, 1350–51, 1352–53, 1353, 1370–71, 1376, 1378.

1 January: Rushworth, VII, 1380 (with *CJ*, VI, 107), 1380–81, 1381, 1381–82.

2 January: Rushworth, VII, 1382.

3 January: Rushworth, VII, 1382–83, 1383.

4 January: Rushworth, VII, 1383–84 (with *CJ*, VI, 111).

5 January: *CJ*, VI, 111.

6 January: Rushworth, VII, 1384, 1384–85; Nalson, 1–4; Rushworth, VII, 1385, 1385.

8 January: *CJ*, VI, 113–14; Nalson, 5–7.

9 January: Rushworth, VII, 1387, 1387, 1387, 1388–89.

10 January: Rushworth, VII, 1389, 1389, 1389.

11 January: Rushworth, VII, 1389–90.

12 January: Nalson, 11–13.

13 January: Nalson, 14–15.

15 January: Rushworth, VII, 1391, 1391–92.

16 January: Rushworth, VII, 1392, 1392–93.

17 January: Nalson, 17–20, 20.

18 January: Rushworth, VII, 1394; Nalson, 21; Rushworth, VII, 1394.

19 January: Rushworth, VII, 1395, 1395; *Agreement*, 3–6, 7–8, 8, 8, 16–17, 21–22, 22–24, 24–25, 25.

20 January: Rushworth, VII, 1398; Nalson, 24, 25; *KCT*, 9–24; Rushworth, VII, 1395, 1399.

22 January: Rushworth, VII, 1399, 1400; Nalson, 38–39; *KCT*, 25–33; Nalson, 47–49.

23 January: Rushworth, VII, 1404; Nalson, 50–51; *KCT*, 33–41; Nalson, 54–55.

24 January: Rushworth, VII, 1406; *KCT*, 41.

25 January: Rushworth, VII, 1415; Nalson, 62–63, 63–79, 79–82.

26 January: *CJ*, VI, 123; Nalson, 83.

27 January: Nalson, 85, 86–92, 93, 94–103 (Nalson embroidering upon *KCT*, 42–73); *KCT*, 52–69 (with corrections and additions from the more polished text in Muddiman, 114–25); Rushworth, VII, 1421, 1421, 1421.

29 January: Rushworth, VII, 1427, 1427, 1427 (with Firth & Rait, I, 1262–63), 1428; Nalson, 105–6, 108–11; Rushworth, VII, 1428, 1428.

30 January: Firth & Rait, I, 1263–64; *KCT*, 74–83.

Epilogue: *CJ*, VI, 132, 133; Nalson, 118–20.